TAKE FIVE

TAKE FIVE

Devotions
to Strengthen
a Man
in His Work

EDITED BY

ROBERT
BUSHA

BROADMAN
& HOLMAN
PUBLISHERS

Nashville, Tennessee

© 1994
Broadman & Holman Publishers
All rights reserved

Printed in the United States of America

4253-66
0-8054-5366-0

Dewey Decimal Classification: 242.642
Subject Heading: DEVOTIONAL LITERATURE // MEN—RELIGIOUS LIFE
Library of Congress Card Catalog Number: 93-45614

Library of Congress Cataloging-in-Publication Data
Take five! : devotions to strengthen a man in his work / Robert Busha,
editor.
    p. cm.
    ISBN 0-8054-5366-0
    1. Men—Prayer-books and devotions—English. 2.
Work—Religious aspects—Christianity. 3. Christian life—1960–
I. Busha, Robert, 1943– .
BV4843.T354   1994
242'.642—dc20
                                                            93-45614
                                                               CIP

Of the many who have influenced the way I work,
three stand out as distinctive.
This volume of Take Five! is dedicated to them.

First, there is the memory of my father, Bud. By his example he
taught me to work hard and long and to do it honestly.

My first major employer after college,
Congressman William S. Mailliard, by his example,
taught me to work even harder and longer, but to do it smarter.

The third source of influence is having an even greater impact:
God is teaching me that working harder and longer
and even smarter is perhaps commendable, but not necessarily good.
He is patiently showing me that if I simply do His work
He'll take care of mine.
He's also more than willing to set the pace, demanding much,
but never asking more than I am capable of doing.
All I have to do is follow Him and His example.

Acknowledgments

Thanks to the staff at Broadman & Holman Publishers, especially our editor, Janis Whipple, for the opportunity to share; and to my wife, Mary Catherine, my collaborator, editor, and continuing source for support and encouragement.

Contents

Acknowledgments vi

Introduction: Changing Pace / Robert Busha 1

1. Just Silence / John Atherton 3

2. Hallelujah, Anyhow! / Terrence Barrett 5

3. Reaching Mountaintops / Dan Benson 7

4. It's Facing the Wrong Way / Charles W. Blaker 9

5. God's Faithful Work / James E. Bolton 11

6. Why Didn't You Tell Me? / Charles R. Brown 13

7. The Power of Three / Jerry R. Carr 15

8. Even in Samaria / Tom Carter 17

9. Leaning on Him / Tim Coyle 19

10. The Word Became Life / Jack L. Edwards 21

11. Patience Rewarded / Bernard Epperson 23

12. Keep My Spirit Still / James H. Harrison 25

13. Every Minute Counts / David P. Hauk 27

14. Singing in a Strange Land / Jack Hayford 29

15. The Storm Struck / Oren C. House 31

16. Discipline Is Everything! / R. Kent Hughes 33

17. A New Dimension in Spirituality / Bill Hybels 35

18. Words Caught in the Throat / Michael Martin 37

19. The 850 Club / C. S. McMinn 39
20. Doing the Right Thing / Louis Merryman 41
21. Did God Get Tired? / Al Munger 43
22. Job on Jobs / Eric M. Nishimoto. 45
23. How Much Is Too Much? / Lloyd John Ogilvie 47
24. Sabbath Moments / Ron Redmon 49
25. Can You Spare Just Five? / Harold J. Sala 51
26. Mantles and Mentors / Brad Sargent 53
27. I'd Wished I'd Been Fired / Giles Scott 55
28. A Few Good Men / Robert C. Smith 57
29. Battle Ready / John Strubhar 59
30. It's Done! / Paul P. Tell, Jr. 61
31. I Always Wanted to Be a Runner / Richie G. Thomas 63
32. Response—Ability / Ray C. Veal 65
33. Take It to the Bank / Dennis E. Way 67
34. Words Only Whisper / Donald E. White 69
35. The Race of Life / Gene Wilder 71
36. Can a Christian Be a Salesman? / Dick Williams 73
37. Keep Me from Being Crushed / James E. Bolton 75
38. The Weekend Report / Charles R. Brown 77
39. Go Ahead, Ruin My Day / Jerry R. Carr 79
40. New Hope / Bernard Epperson 81
41. A View from the Fortieth Floor / James H. Harrison 83
42. Forgiveness at Work / C. S. McMinn 85
43. Take a Break / Louis Merryman 87
44. Rejected or Renewed? / Al Munger 89
45. Life on a Gridlocked Freeway / Eric M. Nishimoto. 91
46. Winning My Children / Giles Scott 93
47. A Priceless Jewel / John Strubhar 95
48. Foundations for Progress / Paul P. Tell, Jr. 97
49. Those Aggravating Do-Gooders / Richie G. Thomas 99
50. A Record Week / Dennis E. Way 101
51. I Can Still Work on You / Dick Williams 103
52. Agents of Reconciliation / James H. Harrison 105
53. Stop Running and Stopping / Paul P. Tell, Jr. 107
54. Somebody's Watching / Robert Busha 109
    Meet Our Contributors 111
    Credits 117

Therefore comfort one another with these words.

1 Thessalonians 4:18, NASB

Introduction: Changing Pace

We're living in unique times, especially regarding travel and communication. This was particularly well illustrated during the brief military exercise liberating Kuwait in 1991.

Leaders on all sides watched live reports of combat operations and diplomatic forays given by reporters in the field. They received decision-making information faster from the broadcasts of CNN than it could be transmitted through diplomatic and military channels.

Just think about it. Today, it's technologically possible to communicate from any point on the globe to almost any other—and to do it in nearly an instant. Ideas may be shared with people in remote corners and impassable places on mountain, jungle, desert, and urban sites, with the agile assistance of radios, televisions, and audio- and videocassette players. And even though physically getting to any one of these desperate locations may take longer than sending a message, air travel and all-terrain vehicles (mechanical and animal) leave very little of the earth as untouchable.

The consequences are abrupt. The signals cannot be ignored. The pace of life is quickening. Many of us are caught in a daily flurry of activity. We're trying to do more in less time. And we're unconsciously absorbing an urgency to do even more. Just do it faster!

Be productive. Be efficient. Be effective. Be as useful as technology will permit: portable phones, hand-held TVs, pocket computers, satellite feeds, microwave relays, conference calls, go, go, go—stop!

Now, mentally step back a moment and accept another, more soothing, thought.

An increasing number of us realize that constant motion is not, in and of itself, of value. More is not always better. In order to make the best use of ourselves in concert with the technological innovations at our disposal, our deliberations must become more deliberate; our thinking, more thoughtful; our actions, more consciously acted out. We can still be creative and make rapid, intuitive, and computer-assisted decisions, but we can do it more sensibly, yes, even more productively.

This perspective emphasizes the value of reflection. We can enhance our effectiveness and bring greater value to our lives by setting aside precious moments to prayerfully consider our definition of success, our goals, our objectives, and how to keep our responsibilities in balance.

"Take five" to read and reflect on the devotions that follow. Do it every day and your life will never be the same.

Robert Busha

Father,

Help me overcome my tendency to work without You

unless I'm in trouble. Teach me to keep You in my day, all day.

I know You're in mine. Guide my choices, direct my walk,

let me see Your way for me. And, Lord, please let these shared words

comfort and inspire my brothers everywhere.

Amen.

Just Silence

John Atherton

"I gotta go," I called to my wife as I rushed out the door on my way to the office. *I'm going to be late again,* I thought, reaching in my pocket for the car keys.

The sun was barely up and already my mind was filled with projects to be completed and people I needed to connect with. As my mind raced to figure out how I was going to get everything done, I turned the key in the ignition switch. There was a long silence. I tried again. The result was the same. *Great,* I thought, *I'm already late and now I have a dead battery.* With the help of some jumper cables and an "I'll deal with this later" approach, I was off to the office.

When I arrived, I found two people who both had an eight o'clock appointment waiting to see me. I spoke briefly to one, rescheduling our appointment for lunch, while almost simultaneously inviting the other one to have a seat in my office.

As I sat down at my desk my eyes caught sight of a note that simply read, "I'll be by around eight-thirty and I'd like a copy of the report." I knew my appointment would run past eight-thirty, so I left a note on my office door that I would bring the report by on my way to my luncheon appointment.

While meeting with my eight o'clock appointment I noticed a note being slipped under the door. Knowing it must be something important, I excused myself long enough to read it. The message: "The phones are down."

As I was finishing up with my appointment, my mind was occupied with a report that needed to be prepared and phone lines that were critical to our operation, but not available. To top things off, after walking my appointment to the door, I returned to find a fax note that my eleven o'clock meeting had been moved to ten o'clock and asking if I could make it? After a quick phone call from another office regarding our telephone lines, I grabbed the report and headed for the door. As I hopped into my car I prayed, "Lord, please let this car start. I'm late."

There was a long silence from the car, but this time I sensed the Lord saying to me, "Slow down, John!"

Lord,

thank You for reminding me

how easy it is for my life to be controlled by my circumstances.

Help me to choose to move beyond them

by acknowledging that You have everything under control

and that my business is often a hindrance

to what You want to accomplish in and through me.

Amen.

And we know that God causes all things to work together
for good to those who love God,
to those who are called according to His purpose.

Romans 8:28, NASB

Hallelujah, Anyhow!

Terrence Barrett

It seems as if yesterday's story has barely ended before today's battle begins. The loud, penetrating buzzer of the alarm clock harshly intrudes into my bedroom, gleefully snatches back the covers of slumber, and shouts, "Wake up, it's time to go to work!"

My memory bank pours out painful pictures of yesterday: *Why did I make such a stupid comment in that meeting? How did I completely forget about that appointment? Where did I put that document?* In the meantime, my imagination draws a discouraging picture of what lies ahead: meaningless paperwork, trivial telephone calls, rushed deadlines—not to mention that task I've volunteered to take that no one else would touch. The bad news is sometimes I feel like just giving up. And the good news is that I can!

I can give it up to God! "Casting all your anxiety upon Him, because He cares for you" (1 Pet. 5:7). I've carried my own burdens long enough! God is saying, "Allow me to accomplish what you cannot." I've realized that God doesn't want me to be Him, just His child.

Many of us are trying to do for ourselves what God said He would do. God didn't tell us to supply our own needs; He said He would (Phil. 4:19). God didn't tell us to work it out for our own good; He said He would (Rom. 8:28). God didn't tell us to exalt ourselves; He said He would (Luke 14:11). However, God did call us to humble ourselves and trust in Him.

Jeremiah 17:7 says, "Blessed is the man who trusts in the Lord and whose trust is the Lord." The Bible says to "Consider it all joy...when you encounter various trials, knowing that the testing of your faith produces endurance. And let endurance have its perfect result, that you may be perfect and complete, lacking in nothing" (Jas. 1:2–4). So by faith, I choose to consider today a joy, even though I may be facing frustrating situations, for I know that God is doing something wonderful in my life. He's teaching me something I need to know, as I cast my anxieties on Him.

As the old songs says, "When misfortunes come your way, lift your hands to God and say hallelujah, anyhow!"

Dear Lord,

thank You for being my Father.

Thank You for guiding me in the direction of Your perfect purpose,

so that You can teach me, mold me,

and shape me into that which is pleasing to You.

As You do Your work in my life—

Lord, no matter how uncomfortable it may feel—

I want to continually praise You.

In Jesus' name I pray.

Amen.

Great are the works of the Lord:
they are pondered by all who delight in them.
Glorious and majestic are his deeds.

Psalm 111:2–3, NIV

Reaching Mountaintops

Dan Benson

Sometimes I become so focused on an objective that it's as if I'm wearing a set of invisible blinders. Nothing can distract me.

While climbing mountains, I used to be so focused on reaching the summit that I would fix my eyes on the dirt path just a few feet in front of me, place one boot in front of the other, and suffer all kinds of agony in order to "make good time" up the mountain. Stop and rest? We'll rest when we get there! Admire the view? Just wait till we get to the top!

One bright Colorado October day, a couple of friends and I set out for the top of Long's Peak. But after we had hiked an hour or so, our pristine blue sky was suddenly elbowed aside by a horde of angry, black storm clouds. Within moments we were engulfed by thick fog and icy snow. Our eyes stung as high winds whipped the snow into our faces. Before long we were walking in several inches of snow—and the storm was just beginning.

For a while we actually enjoyed the macho adventure of climbing onward and upward through the hostile elements. But when the storm showed no sign of letting up, we admitted we had to turn back. Stronger climbers had lost their lives on this mountain, in storms just like this one. So, reluctantly, we turned around and trudged down the mountain. We had set out for the peak and were denied.

But as we descended to our campsite, something dawned on me. Although we had missed the summit, this was quite an adventure! My friends and I were having a great time. It was an opportunity to blow urban soot out of our lungs, drink in the sights and smells of God's creation, get some high-altitude exercise, talk and laugh together, and, yes—even pay our humble respects to the majestic wrath of a Rocky Mountain snowstorm.

I was actually enjoying myself. As we tramped and laughed our way down the mountain, I began to realize that the trip wasn't a failure; it was a smashing success.

Father,

give me the vision to set the summit as my destination,

the strength to make the journey,

and the peace to enjoy each and every step of the way with You.

Amen.

He leads me beside still waters;

He restores my soul.

Psalm 23:2–3, NRSV

It's Facing the Wrong Way

Charles W. Blaker

While serving as headmaster of a Presbyterian boarding school in Maryland, I made a whopping discovery: My desk faced the wrong way!

My office at the academy included a bay window with a clear view across the campus. For nearly four years I sat behind that desk with the window at my back. In front of me was a wall with a door. Through the door came people—quite a lot of people. Most of them had some problem the headmaster was supposed to be able to solve.

After a few years of this kind of thing you begin to believe that life is like the fishbowl at the county fair. Only the packages are not little prizes but little troubles. You pay your dime and you drop in your line. The lucky headmaster is the one who finds the smallest package of trouble tied to his hook!

I had been wallowing in that cynical mood for an hour, trying to complete a writing project that was already two days past deadline. In disgust, I finally crumpled the paper, swung around in my swivel chair, and glared out the window.

The evening sunset had a luminous quality in which everything seemed to float in a sea of gold. Down by the lake a young couple strolled. The willow trees on the far bank of the lake seemed to grow out of the trunks of their inverted images mirrored in the still water.

I guess it's because I spent all my early years in the concrete jungle of a big city that woods, fields, and bodies of water still seemed so enchanting to me. I remember that when I first saw the Atlantic Ocean, I couldn't get enough of it. So the lake outside my office window was very special to me. And this particular evening the view of the lake provided a special lesson.

Many of us spend most of our lives looking the wrong way. We become petty, often cynical, reflecting the trivialities of our daily concerns. And sometimes behind us, if we would only turn around, is the vast sweep of the eternal divine wonder, the gift of the Creator for those with the eyes to see.

Memo to the custodial staff the following day: "Please turn headmaster's desk around!"

Father,
sometimes I grow cynical and petty.
Help me take the time to look around my life,
to appreciate Your creation.
Amen.

While the earth remains,
seedtime and harvest, and cold and heat,
and summer and winter,
and day and night shall not cease.

Genesis 8:22, NASB

God's Faithful Work

James E. Bolton

"Winter's coming," I said. The weather report I was listening to brought dire promises of frost and possible snow. And with that report, another realization: *I need to bring in what is left in my garden before the frost ruins them.*

As I picked the remaining vegetables, I thought about the comparisons between how God works in the cycles of the seasons and how He works in my life.

In springtime, God brings a renewal of the earth from the deadness of winter just as He brings a renewal to my life after I ask Him to forgive me for breaking His rules and rebelling against Him.

The way that I plant my crops in summer is similar to how God plants His seed in me as I read His Word and listen to His voice.

In autumn, I harvest my crops and enjoy what the garden has produced, in just the same way God uses the growth and talents that He's given me to further His kingdom and then enjoys all that He has produced.

Finally, as the cold and snowy weather of winter brings a time of rest to the earth, God brings a time of rest in Him in preparation for future growth.

Through seeing how God works in each of these seasons, I have learned how God can be depended upon to bring the earth through each cycle.

Likewise, I've also seen how I can depend on God to bring me through each cycle of my life. This includes those times when so much was going wrong that my life seemed to be in total chaos.

During times of great stress, I'm so glad I can depend on God to fulfill His promises. He who began His good work in me will continue to perfect it until Jesus comes again.

Thank You, God,
that You are faithful to Your work in the earth
and in me.
Amen.

Always be prepared to give an answer
to everyone who asks you to give the reason
for the hope that you have.

1 Peter 3:15, NIV

Why Didn't You Tell Me?

Charles R. Brown

The art class at our community college proved to be great fun. Creative juices flowed freely, and I lapped up the praise from my instructor like a thirsty dog that had just crossed a desert.

I had the opportunity to experiment with all kinds of tools that were new to me. I learned many new things about the wonderful world of art. However, it was several months after the class started that I learned something that caused me to do some serious thinking about my faith.

In class I talked casually to a number of people, but most of the time I kept to myself and made my way home as soon as the class ended.

During this same time my wife and I had become involved in a young and growing church. We were encouraged and challenged as we watched others reaching out to people with the message of Christ.

It wasn't long before our friends, Wayne and Colleen, introduced us to a neighbor they'd led to the Lord. To my surprise it was one of the other students in my art class.

Soon after our introduction this new Christian asked, "Charlie, why didn't you tell me?" She was one of the people I casually greeted each week in class. In fact, I sat beside her. I shared art supplies with her. We talked about the routine stuff of life, but I never really got to know her and her need.

"Why didn't you tell me?" she asked.

If a soul could perspire mine surely did. And she asked me that question at church, too. There in midst of the place that represented all of the reason for my living, she asked why I hadn't said anything to her about God.

You see, I don't like to make waves. I suppose that's why I felt so convicted when confronted with her question. Jesus made waves—a lot of waves. He calmed waves, too. Just as He told the sea to be still, He speaks to the inner storms that rush through the lives of people around me.

Men, I have to be honest with you. There are times when I need to confess that I really don't seem to care. At least my priorities in life appear to demonstrate that I don't care about the eternal destiny of other souls. But I do care. I really care. And I realize I have a responsibility to demonstrate the blessing God brings to my life by sharing it with others.

Great Calmer of my soul,
grant to me a renewed desire to tell others
and to be ready to give an answer
for the hope that is mine in Christ Jesus.
Amen.

Two are better than one…if either of them falls, the one will lift up his companion. But woe to the one who falls when there is not another to lift him up…
A cord of three strands is not quickly torn apart.

Ecclesiastes 4:9–12, NASB

The Power of Three

Jerry R. Carr

One of America's great idols has fallen on its face, similar to the fall of Dagon the national god of the Philistines in 1 Samuel 5:3. This idol is the idol of security apart from God. Americans have typically found an artificial security in working for large companies, accumulating wealth through insurance programs, retirement programs, and so on. But with the fall of so many corporate giants, the continual cut-backs in companies across the nation, inflation, escalating medical costs (I think you get the picture), even the most affluent among us are beginning to wonder if there really is a place of safety in the midst of all the chaos.

As believers in Jesus Christ, we know that the only real place of security is in God. But as the fallout continues, it is apparent that hardships are falling on the just as well as the unjust.

As I've watched this phenomenon, I've noticed something very wonderful and something very sad. So what could be wonderful about what I have just described? In the midst of difficult circumstances many believers are discovering the wonderful support that comes from living in relationship with Jesus Christ and other believers. When life gets you down it really helps to know you have a mighty God who loves you, and brothers and sisters who are there to help lift you up.

Sadly, not all believers take advantage of this wonderful gift in the body of Christ. Instead of receiving God's comfort, counsel, and encouragement through Christian fellowship, some choose to live in isolation, to tough it out on their own. Because of His grace, I'm sure that God will meet us in our place of isolation, but how much better when we fulfill the "one anothers" of Scripture and minister and receive grace and edification, in the name of Jesus.

Brothers, when will we ever learn that we need one another? When will we repent of the macho foolishness that isolates us from one another? Isn't it about time we prove how strong we really are by tearing down the walls we hide behind and letting the real people behind the walls be known? I don't know about you, but when I'm in a world of hurt, I'm glad there's a world of encouragement in our Lord Jesus Christ and His Church.

Father,
thank You for the wonderful gifts You have given me
in my brothers and sisters in Christ.
Help me each day to break out
from behind my walls of isolation
into a new life of vital relationships.
Lord, I thank You, also,
that every relationship I build with a brother and a sister in Christ
is a relationship of three,
because You join us each time we gather.
Amen.

But you shall receive power
when the Holy Spirit has come upon you;
and you shall be My witnesses both in Jerusalem, and in all Judea
and Samaria,
and even to the remotest part of the earth.

Acts 1:8, NASB

Even in Samaria

Tom Carter

In my first year of pastoral ministry I preached on Acts 1:8. I showed how Jesus commissioned His disciples to take His good news to ever-widening areas: First the city of Jerusalem, then the regions of Judea and Samaria, finally the remotest part of the earth.

I explained that for centuries Samaria had been enemy territory for the Jews. In Old Testament accounts, Jews had no dealings with the Samaritans. Yet Jesus told His men to take the gospel message even to these people.

I asked my congregation, "Who is your Samaritan, your worst enemy? Whoever it is, Christ expects you to witness even to that person."

The next week a police officer in our congregation confessed he hated the people who lived in the high-crime area he patrolled.

"While you were preaching last week," he told me, "God made me see that these people were my Samaritans." Then he took me out to the parking lot. He'd made a sign and posted it on the dashboard inside his patrol car. The sign read, "You shall be My witness in Samaria."

17

Since then, I've read Acts 1:8 dozens of times. I'm often reminded of that police officer and how God used the simple proclamation of His Word to speak to this man's heart and change his life.

Sometimes people who listen to my sermons respond in ways more dramatic than that, usually much less, and often I see no visible fruit at all. But that one encounter forever taught me that God will always honor His Word. That encourages me to keep sharing it.

Father God,
build in me faithfulness to Your Word,
whether or not I see its fruit.
Thanks for the encouragement You often give me,
but keep me steadfast even when everything looks discouraging.
Through Christ my Lord,
Amen.

Trust in the Lord with all your heart,
and do not lean on your own understanding.
In all your ways acknowledge Him,
and He will make your paths straight.

Proverbs 3:5–6, NASB

Leaning on Him

Tim Coyle

An annual retreat I attend was recently held at a camp that borders on the Appalachian Trail. I've always wanted to walk the Trail, so this particular site promised to be an added bonus to the retreat. Soon after we arrived, a friend of mine and I decided to go for a hike.

Because it follows the crest of the mountain, the trail itself is a smooth and level walk. But the way up to it is a challenge. We followed a path that worked its way through a hardwood forest, which then gave way to a blanket of pine trees. The last few hundred yards were especially tough. The incline was steep, and in addition to the pine trees, the hillside was covered with rocks and boulders. We made it, though, and the view from an observation point along the trail was breathtaking.

We spent a long time there, sitting and talking and enjoying the beauty of God's creation. Then we started back. To our surprise, the way down turned out to be even more difficult than the way up. It was hard to keep from falling forward. I must have looked something like a crab because I was on all fours, but face up. Yet it was the only way I could keep my balance. My friend, however, was having virtually no trouble at all. Because of a bad knee he was walking with a cane, and it served him well.

He suggested I grab a stick to use. With all the pine trees around, it wasn't difficult to find one. As I began to walk with it, I couldn't believe the difference. Not only could I stand upright, but as I leaned on the stick I could easily find my next step without the fear of falling.

That experience reminded us both of the place that God wants to have in our lives. God knows that we don't do very well in this life on our own. Therefore, He offers us His divine direction and help through His Word. Although we may have confidence in our own resources, they're no match for what He can provide. He lovingly invites us to lean on Him and to draw from His wisdom. If we will, He promises to lead us in the finest life possible.

Father,
thank You for loving me enough
to provide Your wisdom for me through Your Word.
Help me to think less of my own abilities
so I can make full use of what You offer me.
Amen.

Never will I forsake you.

Hebrews 13:5, NIV

The Word Became Life

Jack L. Edwards

Suddenly, I became aware of the radio dispatcher's voice projecting a sense of urgency as she repeatedly called: "Seventeen-ten; seventeen-ten!"

I was en route to work as an auto theft investigator for the California Highway Patrol. As I drove along in my unmarked highway patrol vehicle, my mind recalled what had been said in church the night before. The preacher had said that Jesus would never forsake me and that He'd always be with me. But I was struggling with so many issues: How do I know if Jesus has really come into my heart? How can I be sure? How can I know that this is all true? It just didn't seem logical. And since I couldn't see Jesus, it didn't seem possible. How could I know for sure?

And then I realized that a brother officer had not responded to the dispatcher, and since I was approaching beat "Ten," I radioed my location and offered to help. The message was urgent: "A suspected drunk driver is weaving on and off sidewalks and front lawns in a nearby neighborhood and numerous mothers are calling in fear of school children being run over."

I took the next highway off ramp and soon located the suspect vehicle parked at a curb. I approached the driver and immediately recognized him, calling him by name. Extremely intoxicated, but docile and friendly, I remembered booking him over a year ago for drunk driving.

After a few minutes and the arrival of the beat officer, a city police officer, a deputy sheriff, and a tow truck driver, I heard my name being called from the porch of a nearby house. "Good morning, Jack. Good job," the lady hollered.

It was at that instant that the Holy Spirit "zapped" my heart, as I realized that all of the officers, the tow truck driver, and the lady on the porch were all Christians. Since that moment I have never questioned the truth that Jesus would always be with me. That was over twenty-two years ago.

Thank You, Lord,
for revealing Yourself to me in such a graphic way.
You are the Way, the Truth, and the Life.
You really do love and care for me,
and will always be there for me,
anytime, anywhere—even on the job.
Amen.

For the anger of man
does not achieve the righteousness of God.

James 1:20, NASB

Patience Rewarded

Bernard Epperson

Anger had always been a problem for me. I'd been cursed with a terrible temper even as a child. When I turned to the Lord, controlling that temper was one of the first things I prayed about. I asked God to replace my anger with His peace. This prayer was constantly in the back of my mind.

There was a man at work named John. He wasn't a Christian and saw no reason at all to keep his temper under control. The slightest thing would send him into fits of rage.

"Get angry," he used to tell me. "It's good for you."

But I always remembered the verse from James. I knew my anger would not allow things to be done the way God wanted them done. I wanted to show people peace and joy.

Despite John's attitude, I worked hard to be patient and tried to speak gently. At times it was very difficult, and I'd become so frustrated that I'd have to slip away and pray silently for a few moments to quiet my spirit. But I kept at it.

One day John had a bad tantrum. He screamed and cursed at his coworkers and stomped out. In the past he'd always been forgiven and permitted to return to work the next day, but this time he was fired. To my surprise the supervisor offered me John's job. He said they'd seen my hard work and good attitude and thought I'd be the right person to move up.

That night I thanked God for all He'd done in my heart. He rewarded me for my efforts, and I knew He'd continue to help me beat my temper if I gave it up to Him.

Lord,
thank You for working in my life
and helping me overcome my temper
in order to show others Your peace.
Amen.

The Lord answered her,
"Martha, Martha, you are worried and distracted by many things;
there is need of only one thing."

Luke 10:41–42, NRSV

Keep My Spirit Still

James H. Harrison

Time management, or lack of it, is one of the biggest stressors in our fast-paced, do-it-all society.

While attending seminary, I pastored a church in a small town. My days were full and hectic, especially during Advent and Christmas. I recall one year clearly, preparing for holiday services. Realizing that I had misplaced the file with my ideas, liturgies, music, and sermon notes, I frantically began to search my office for the missing file. While searching, a friend, the police chief, walked in for a cup of coffee and a chat. He noticed my frantic state. Telling him about my dilemma, I added that I really didn't have time to visit. The chief calmly said, "You may not have time, but it sure seems necessary."

I stood straight up and quietly admitted, "You're right! It is."

During our visit we shared feelings about the message of Jesus' birth and how it had changed our lives. It calmed me down enough to retrace my steps of the last evening and morning, and I finally found that all-important file. My spirit had been calmed and I was at peace.

Many years have passed and many things have changed, yet for me two things remain constant: time management, or the lack of it; and, no matter how frantic a day may be, it's good to stop in the midst of the activities and retrace my steps—to the babe in a Bethlehem manger. It keeps my spirit still.

Dear God,
while everything around me moves so fast,
keep my spirit still
so that I may walk in quiet communion with You.
In the name of Jesus.
Amen.

What good will it be for a man
if he gains the whole world, yet forfeits his soul?...
What can a man give in exchange for his soul?

Matthew 16:26, NIV

Every Minute Counts

David P. Hauk

While watching television one evening, I saw an advertisement for a luxury car. The *attitude* being promoted by that commercial really disturbed me. On the screen was a beautiful black automobile waiting in the rain at a traffic light. People walked past clutching their coats closed and struggled to keep their umbrellas upright in the wind. The voice-over announced, "You're stopped at a red light. It's only twenty seconds. This may be the only time some people see you. How do you want them to remember you?" It was a blatant appeal to the selfish, materialistic side of human nature, another example of the keeping up with the Joneses trap, another pitch to vanity and ego.

Call me crazy, but I don't want to be remembered for driving a luxury sedan, although that's what many people in our society prefer. The message is direct, "You're no good unless you have the best." Following this line of thinking, our social and professional value depends on the size of our house or the type of car we drive. We're not considered successful unless we have the right material possessions.

Can we be successful without being prosperous? Is there anything more worthwhile to be remembered for than possessions?

How about the way we live? Wouldn't it be better to be remembered for helping people? How about for encouraging others in times of despair? How about feeding the hungry, for clothing the naked, or for visiting those in hospitals and prisons? Would we like to be remembered for reaching out to those who are less fortunate? In short, for showing love to those around us?

Maybe that car commercial was good for something after all. It certainly didn't make me want to go right out and spend more than a year's income for a car. It did remind me that every minute of my life should be a reflection of my love for, and my faith in, God. Because one minute of my life may be the only time people see me and the example I set.

How do you want to be remembered?

Lord,

help me remember that people are watching how I live my life.

May my actions be worthy of You.

Amen.

By the rivers of Babylon,
there we sat down and wept when we remembered Zion.
Upon the willows in the midst of it we hung our harps.
For...how can we sing the Lord's song in a foreign land?

Psalm 137:1,2,4, NASB

Singing in a Strange Land

Jack Hayford

When I was five years old, my family's move from southern California caused me to leave all my friends. We settled in Montana and I entered first grade, adjusting fairly quickly even though being the "new kid on the block" is never easy. Then, about the time I was feeling that Montana was home, we moved again—this time to Oakland, California—and I had to go through the adjustment process once more.

Life stabilized, and by the time I made it to the fifth grade, among my "credits" was membership in the traffic patrol—jaunty hats and sweater stripes and all! But wait! Now on the brink of sixth grade and student office, we moved across town, and there went my friends and status. Later, after becoming a pretty fair basketball player, an injured knee broke my hope of high school stardom.

How often life's moves and changes put us in a strange land. But hear the psalmist, for he also understands: How difficult to sing the Lord's song in a strange land, when things become "foreign" to our plans. This psalm probably refers to the season of exile the kingdom of Judah

29

experienced as many were led captive to Babylon due to the nation's disobedience. No doubt you may well identify with them, for there are enough moves, upset situations, and broken families in our own world for many of us to feel muted—not really ready to sing—silenced in new surroundings.

Disappointing transitions and setbacks and strange settings can spin our plans around, and set our life askew. Life doesn't always work out the way it appeared it might. But our real challenge is to not let circumstances set boundaries that seem to block our prayers and thwart our attempts to continue in the song and spirit of praise. Worship frees us from such boundaries!

O God everywhere present,
I praise You for being available
regardless of time and place and circumstance.
Help me to be at home in Your world, wherever I am,
so I may be faithful in praise
in season and out of season, full or in need, near or far.
Through Christ my Lord,
Amen.

But the ship was now in the midst of the sea,
tossed with waves:
for the wind was contrary.

Matthew 14:24, KJV

The Storm Struck

Oren C. House

Although the twelve disciples were obeying Jesus when they launched their boat out on the blue Sea of Galilee that night, their journey was not to be peaceful. The storm struck with tremendous fury. Waves crashed over their little craft as it tossed helplessly about. Would they perish, abandoned by their Master?

Being in God's will doesn't guarantee our lives will be without trouble, and Jesus often seems to be especially far away when our storms break. But He brought the twelve through the storm safely; He will do the same for us. He hasn't changed.

He seemed remote to me when the company I had served faithfully for fifteen years was sold. At age fifty I was involuntarily forced into job hunting for several months. Had God abandoned me? Clearly, the answer was no! He saw me through the storm.

My wife went back to work and was very supportive throughout the entire ordeal. Fellow Christians undergirded us with prayer and job leads. And my new position supported us until retirement. God has infinite

31

ways to calm our storms. Many times during that period Jesus drew near, lifting our spirits, assuring us of His presence. He will draw near to all who call on Him. With Him, we will ride out every storm. In whatever way our individual storms may end, He will give peace and comfort. His solution is always best.

Lord,
as I face life's inevitable storms,
help me remember that You will never leave me
regardless of my circumstances or how I feel.
Amen.

There is no one righteous,

not even one...

and the way of peace they do not know.

Romans 3:10,17, NIV

Discipline Is Everything!

R. Kent Hughes

Sometime in the early summer before entering the seventh grade, I wandered over from the baseball field and picked up a tennis racket for the first time...and I was hooked!

It was not long before I became a ten-year-old tennis bum. My passion for the sport became so intense that I would idly hold a tennis ball and just sniff it. The *pssst* and the rubbery fragrance of opening a can of new tennis balls became intoxicating. The *whop, whop* and the lingering ring of a sweetly hit ball, especially in the quietness of early morning, was to me symphonic. My memories of this and the summer that followed are of blistering black tennis courts, hot feet, salty sweat, long drafts of delicious rubbery tepid water from an empty ball can, the short shadows of midday heading slowly toward the east, followed by the stadium "daylight" of the court's lights, and the ubiquitous, eerie night bats dive-bombing our lobs.

That fall I determined to become a tennis player. I spent my hoarded savings on one of those old, beautifully laminated David Imperial tennis rackets—a treasure that I actually took to bed with me. I was disciplined! I played every day after school (except during basketball season) and every weekend. When spring came, I biked to the courts where the local high school team practiced and longingly watched until they finally gave in and let me play with them. The next two summers I took lessons, played some tournaments, and practiced about six to eight hours a day—coming home only when they turned off the lights.

And I became good. Not only did I play at a high level, I learned that personal discipline is the indispensable key for accomplishing anything in life.

We will never get anywhere in life without discipline, be it in the arts, business, athletics, or academics. This is doubly so in spiritual matters. In other areas we may be able to claim some innate advantage. An athlete may be born with a strong body, a musician with perfect pitch, or an artist with an eye for perspective. But none of us can claim an innate spiritual advantage. In reality, we are all equally disadvantaged. None of us naturally seeks after God, none is inherently righteous, none instinctively good. Therefore, as children of grace, our spiritual discipline is everything.

I repeat…discipline is everything!

Father,
guide me, coach me, lead me,
and instill in me the focus and determination
to be more like You every hour of every day.
Amen.

Where your treasure is,
there your heart will be also.

Matthew 6:21, NIV

A New Dimension in Spirituality

Bill Hybels

I backed my car out of the driveway as I do every day at 5:45 A.M. While I drove through the neighboring subdivision, I mentally critiqued the architecture. I bought coffee at the twenty-four-hour coffee shop and avoided the talkative cashier. As I turned into the church campus, I formulated a convincing defense for a ministry plan I hoped the staff would adopt. I climbed the stairs to my third-floor office, and wondered at the productivity of the maintenance crew. I shuffled through the mountain of mail on my desk and wished someone else could answer it.

I spun my chair around and looked out the window at the church lake, steaming in the crispness of the morning. In that quiet moment I saw the previous quarter hour for what it had been—an hour tainted by purely human perspective. Not once during that hour had I seen the world through godly eyes. I had thought more about houses than the people inside them. I had considered the tasks awaiting me more important than the woman who served my coffee. I had been more intent on logically supporting my plans than sincerely seeking God's. I'd thought more about staff members' productivity than their walk with the Lord or their family life. I'd viewed correspondence as a drudgery rather than a way to offer encouragement, counsel, or help.

It was only 6:15 A.M. and I needed a renewed heart and mind. Like a compass out of adjustment, my thoughts and feelings were pointing in the wrong direction. They needed to be recalibrated—to be realigned with God's accurate, perfect perspective.

You see, in the space of a day my relationship with Jesus Christ can fall from the heights to the depths, from vitality to superficiality, from life-changing interaction to meaningless ritual. That's a humbling admission, but it's true. I began to pray for guidance and to experiment with various disciplines that would help me be more consistent.

Over the years, as I traveled and spoke at churches and conferences, I occasionally met leaders who somehow seemed to avoid the daily slide into artificial Christianity. Whenever I could, I asked what their secret was. In almost every case, they said "journaling."

I decided to try it. I've never written anything profound, but in simple terms I've chronicled the activity of God in my life, relationships, marriage, children, and ministry. I've also worked through feelings, confronted fears, and weighed decisions. And I've slowed down enough to meet with God.

Lord God,

even though I repeat the same mistakes again and again,

please know that I am continuing to work at being more worthy.

You know that I continue to make decisions inconsistent with my

professed values, but help me stay on track with my intentions.

Help me keep my life under close examination.

Help me to live by Your example.

Amen.

Now then go,
and I, even I, will be with your mouth,
and teach you what you are to say.

Exodus 4:12, NASB

Words Caught in the Throat

Michael Martin

The clock on the classroom wall ticked loudly in the thickening silence as the other students looked at me with impatient eyes. I knew the answer. It was there, somewhere deep down inside me, but I couldn't get it out. The professor waited patiently for what seemed an eternity, but eventually looked to another student for the answer. I was deeply embarrassed.

As I left the classroom in frustration, I thought about how my self-consciousness silenced me. Why did I so often fail when I tried to express publicly what I knew and believed? Was it because I was afraid I'd make a mistake? Was I so afraid that others would disapprove that I dared not speak with conviction? Or did I lack confidence in what it was I claimed to believe to be the truth? There was an example for me in Moses.

When the Lord called on Moses to tell the Israelites of their promised deliverance from Egypt, he lacked self-confidence. He was afraid he'd be unable to convince them that God had appeared to him. Perhaps he even wondered if he could believe what God told him. But God assured him

---

37

that He would be with him and would teach him what to say. With that assurance Moses gained confidence in his ability to communicate what he knew to be the truth.

With God's help I began to understand that my lack of confidence prevented me from fulfilling one of God's promises. Just as with Moses, I know the Lord has a purpose for me. When I'm so self-conscious that I fail to speak my convictions, I withhold from the world something that He intended me to give. When I realize I'm acting as an agent of God, my reservations dissipate and I become confident that I am a messenger of the truth.

Heavenly Father,
give me the courage to carry out Your will
by speaking the truth that You have placed in my heart.
Amen.

The effective prayer of a righteous man
can accomplish much.

James 5:16, NASB

The 850 Club

C. S. McMinn

Work—some people just don't seem to get it or, at least, enough of it. No matter what you do to help, they mess up, drop the ball, or get sick.

I had tried everything to get John a job. For a while we worked together, then he injured his back. So his wife worked while he stayed home to watch their kids. Financially, they limped along. I bought tires and food and gave encouragement. Most of all, I prayed desperately, "Lord, how long?"

Poverty seemed to be their lot in life. They were honest, loving, dedicated saints who bounced checks by mistake. They forgot to pay their phone bill and couldn't afford the reconnection charges. So I helped out...again. I was sick of it.

Finally, a real opportunity came along. A secure government right-up-his-street job. I prayed; I mean, I prayed. I got down on my face before the Lord and something miraculous happened. He said, "Yes, I hear you." I absolutely knew John had that job. I was so confident, I even stuck my neck out and told him so.

Months of interviews followed. John was one of the finalists. I waited. Praying again seemed pointless. When God hears, you know He hears, so why repeat it. At last, the decision arrived. Stunned, I heard the news: no job!

A mixture of fury, despair, and bitterness welled up inside me. I seethed, yelled, even muttered under my breath, "Lord, you promised. I just knew he had the job. I don't care what You have to do; break a leg, send someone overseas (I was desperate). John had that job."

Two agonizing weeks passed. Resentment finally turned to contrition as the Lord led me to 1 Kings 18, where Jezebel had raised up 850 prophets of Baal, and Elijah must have prayed against each one. How had Elijah felt? It would be something like seeing Congress hire almost a thousand witches to pervert America!

And then I understood. Prayers are not wasted. God inhales every supplication (Rev. 5:8). They become a part of His breath, like a mighty wave, ready to strike the shore. For Elijah, the beach was Mt. Carmel. There, all his prayers for justice were released. I, too, must wait like Elijah.

The next day John called. Guess what? Something amazing had happened. By some miracle the job was his!

Joy and thankfulness filled my heart. Prayer, against all odds, had triumphed. I learned a valuable lesson and became a new member of the 850 Club.

Father,

help me to pray through adversity and despair,

knowing that, like Elijah,

the timing of Your answer is ordained to bring the greatest victory.

Amen.

What do you think? There was a man who had two sons.
He went to the first and said,
"Son, go and work today in the vineyard."
"I will not," he answered,
but later he changed his mind and went.

Matthew 21:28–29, NIV

Doing the Right Thing

Louis Merryman

When relatives invited me to the high school graduation ceremony for their children, I wondered why it was being held at a school other than the one they attended. The explanation was simple. During their freshman and sophomore years they'd goofed off and wound up having less then the necessary credits for graduation. They recognized the possible penalties for not having a high school diploma so they doubled up classes during their senior year.

During the day they went to their regular high school. Each evening they went to an *adult* high school, from which they were now scheduled to graduate. I was proud of both of them. They had wised up in time to graduate with their class.

The other graduates at that ceremony had also wised up to the need for a high school diploma. For some, it had taken several years to arrive at this night. Many were married with children. But all had returned to school with the goal of getting that precious high school diploma. Tonight was their night.

Several graduates shared their stories. While their families cheered, they told of making the big mistake of dropping out of school, paying for that decision with even lower paying jobs, and their struggle to get a diploma. The audience cheered each one as they marched proudly across the stage. Those graduates were all winners. They'd each one finally said yes!

When God gives us a job to do we have a choice. Have you said no to God, or procrastinated in doing something God wants you to do? Now is a good time to get started. It's never too late.

Thank You, Lord,
for giving me the chance to recapture opportunities thought lost,
undo what I have done in haste,
and the time needed to bring Your kingdom closer.
In Jesus' name.
Amen.

And by the seventh day
God completed His work which He had done;
and He rested on the seventh day
from all His work which He had done.

Genesis 2:2, NASB

Did God Get Tired?

Al Munger

I hated to go home. The hurt and anger in my wife's eyes made me feel guilty. Like other workaholics, I halfheartedly vowed—though only to myself—to stay away from the office on my day off. But seven hours later I would head for the church, saying, I'll be back in forty minutes. I just want to write some memos to the staff.

Four, maybe six, hours later I would come home to my sweet, tolerant, forgiving, disappointed, and sometimes, angry spouse. My response was a little controlled resentment and a lot of self-justification. *After all, I'm a pastor; so many people depend on me. Besides, it's the Lord's work.* That always seemed to justify my number one commitment.

I was wrong. Prior to being assigned to His vineyard, I had, willingly and gratefully, accepted the privilege and responsibility of being a husband.

God had declared that I was to love my wife as Christ loved the church and gave Himself up for her. Yet here I was giving more attention to people in the congregation than I was giving my wife.

I was also ignoring another basic command from my heavenly Father, to take a weekly day off and rest. God finished the work of creation in six days and rested on the seventh.

Did God get tired? Or was He modeling the concept of a rest day for future generations? Maybe you thought your day off was a product of some labor union's arbitration. Not so. No one really knows how long those creation days were, but a day of rest was in the original plan for all mankind.

This divine prescription for our health and welfare was illustrated again when God's people were about to enter the Promised Land and were instructed to work the land six years and let it rest every seventh year (Lev. 25:1–4).

Rest day means time with your wife and children. It means putting your feet up, releasing your mind from the urgent and complex demands of your work. See how the Holy Spirit will renew your mind when you take time to converse with the Lord and feed on His Word. New energy, new dreams, and fresh motivation come when we are resting. If God needed a day off, maybe we do too!

How blessed I am, Father,

to have one day each week to rest,

to renew my mind and spirit.

Help me to use this day as You intended,

and may it be a special day for blessing others.

Amen.

Why is life given to a man whose way is hidden,
whom God has hedged in? For sighing comes to me instead of food;
my groans pour out like water. What I feared has come upon me;
what I dreaded has happened to me.
I have no peace, no quietness; I have no rest, but only turmoil.

Job 3:23–26, NIV

Job on Jobs

Eric M. Nishimoto

I lost my life, once, without really dying. I became unemployed. My middle-class world no longer seemed to have any space for me. I was nothing but an ex-up-and-comer who came and went before his time, a sort of disabled veteran of the status-conscious eighties who suddenly couldn't keep up with his peers.

Like Job, I was disillusioned by my loss and befuddled by my God. And, like Job, I had friends and family who were more than willing to clarify things for me in their own terms, yet who only served to intensify my ruinous feelings. I became depressed to the point of inaction, sitting on my own dung pile of emotions and fears. However, unlike Job, God didn't lift me off the heap in glorious affirmation, because I didn't let Him. Rather than turning back to God for strength and perspective, I turned away, afraid of what would come next.

I replaced my faith in God with a misguided hope in my ability to earn back a respectable career. The ironic result was a nosedive in faith, not in Him, but in the false prophet created by my own hands. Not that

I didn't blame God for my problems or constantly question Him about why things didn't seem to be going right.

While asking God why, I completely lost sight of His way. My narrow and selfish focus and my misguided questioning of His purpose and logic made me afraid and distrustful. I fell into deeper depression as I abandoned all hope of gainful employment and self-respect. But our Lord stuck with me anyway and I survived.

It's too bad that our ignorance makes us unable to comprehend God. Because we are so limited, we also limit Him. The desperation and anguish of the moment closes our eyes to the immovable wisdom and infinite strength of God. Instead of all the things we do and try in our vain attempts to control our lives, all we need to do is look up. Too often we focus on the tiny whirlwind we're caught in and not the huge calm surrounding it.

Heavenly Father,
don't let me forget about You,
especially in the hard times
when my own impatience, stupidity, and fear
incline me toward faithlessness and independence from Your way.
Amen.

For the people of this world are more shrewd
in dealing with their own kind
than are the people of the light.

Luke 16:8, NIV

How Much Is Too Much?

Lloyd John Ogilvie

I had a good visit with one of America's most successful businessmen on a cross-country flight recently. He had risen from a very humble background into immense wealth. I asked him the secret of his success. His response was very interesting.

"Shrewdness!" was his one-word reply.

I was shocked by his frankness.

He went on to say that he spent every waking hour thinking, scheming, planning, developing, and putting deals together. In it all, however, he has tried to be completely honest in all his affairs!

I couldn't help but admire his single-mindedness. He knew what he wanted and left nothing to chance. He worked hard to achieve his goals. All the power of his intellect, the strength of his seemingly limitless energies, the determination of his iron will and the resources of his calculated discernment of people were employed to accomplish his goals.

When it seemed natural and unforced, I shifted our conversation into what the man believed about God. There was a long silence. He admitted that he had not taken any time to think about that. He was astonished by my response: "If you ever put the same time, energy, and will into being a disciple of Jesus Christ, you would be a contemporary of the apostle Paul."

The man's response was thoughtful and reflective: "Nobody has ever challenged me with that!"

The conversation with my traveling companion made a deep impression on me. It forced me to wonder if I could say that Jesus Christ meant as much to me as this man's career does to him. That led me into a long analysis of people I know in business, entertainment, government, and sports who invest incalculable personal thought and resources to get ahead. No cost is too high; no sacrifice, too demanding. Scheming, study, rehearsal, practice, and determination are committed as a small price for perfection and success. I often wonder what would happen if Christians took following Jesus Christ as seriously as these people take getting ahead.

Father,
help me to focus daily on following You
with all my determination and all my resources.
Amen.

Be at rest once more,
O my soul, for the Lord has been good to you.
Psalm 116:7, NIV

Sabbath Moments

Ron Redmon

We work diligently to keep the Sabbath for worship, rest, and family recreation. It's the one day of the week we deliberately set aside for recharging our batteries: mentally, physically, and spiritually. It's a time of refreshment. We all need it. I know I sure do.

I'm a registered nurse and I work on an oncology ward. We serve patients of all ages and in all stages of cancer development and treatment. Our work also involves dealing with discomfort, pain, and death—a lot of it. And it's not always easy to handle.

Our nursing team seems to be shorthanded almost all the time. There's always more to do than can reasonably be expected of us. Often there are too many lights flashing—patients wanting someone to come to them—and we're forced to make choices about who gets served first. Who will get our attention? A request for pain medication in one room. The need for a simple drink of water in another. Clean sheets for a wet and soiled bed. Loneliness. Dispair. A friendly touch. A listening ear. Things we thought absolutely *must* be done get dropped further down the list to become just remotely possible accomplishments. Patient needs we couldn't have imagined at the beginning of our shift sometimes take command.

When time seems to be running against us, when we're running short of energy and our wits are getting thin, I try to remember Sundays. I reach back and ahead and remember that Sunday is the day especially for worship and rest. Sunday is the day my family and I look to the Lord with the members of our Christian fellowship and give praise and thanks to Him for all He has provided, for all He will provide. It's the one day of the week I can look to God to remind me I'm not going through life alone. He is with me.

Taking even a brief whisp of time during a weekday to do that same thing is a Sabbath moment for me. A few seconds to celebrate, to give praise, to give thanks. It's also a time I can realize that on the cancer ward we also deal with giving comfort, with relieving pain, and with helping God to give and keep life...and I'm refreshed.

Lord Jesus,
it's so easy to be busy and let the pressures of the moment
push me through the day.
Lord, I confess I have again let myself be distracted from You
by things that seem to be urgent.
Let me enter Your rest at this moment.
Refresh me by still waters.
Then as I resume my day, let me do so yoked with You,
that I might be gentle and humble with You,
that I may be a joy to You.
Amen.

Be very careful, then, how you live…
making the most of every opportunity.

Ephesians 5:15–16, NIV

Can You Spare Just Five?

Harold J. Sala

Okay, you've decided to take five minutes a day to focus on God. So what can you expect?

Very soon you'll discover one of Murphy's Laws. "Anything that can happen, will happen," will seem to have been written with you in mind. In spite of your best intentions, you'll oversleep; you'll discover your socks don't match and the search for a matching pair will use up your five minutes; you'll have extra work that keeps you up late; you'll set the clock to ring early, but an alarm that has never failed before will not go off!

How do I know? I've tried it at least a hundred times. However, I've started at least one-hundred-and-one times, and I don't intend to quit trying. That's why I want to share five simple guidelines to help you develop enough time for spiritual meditation and study.

First, make a commitment to take five minutes a day to be with the Lord. Every journey begins with one step. Your decision to enrich your life by setting aside just three-tenths of one percent of a twenty-four-hour period is the beginning of a journey that *can* change your life.

Second, be specific in scheduling five minutes a day. When is the best time? Anytime, right? Wrong! Practically speaking, anytime is *some other time*, and *some other time* never gets scheduled. Make it a habit at the same time each and every day.

Third, have a plan. Include Scripture, or God's Word in the Bible; it's here we find the strength of the ages, and through these pages He speaks to us. Then, you need moments of reflection or meditation as you ask yourself, "How does this apply to my life? How do I apply this to what I'm facing right now?" You also need a few moments to talk directly to God in prayer. It's during these moments that you'll connect with Him by sharing what's in your heart.

Fourth, stay focused, possibly by reading aloud, or by writing your thoughts in a journal. Make a conscious decision to put your mind where your body is, and worship God.

Fifth, discipline yourself, and if necessary cut something else out of your overburdened schedule. Nobody, including me, can honestly say, "I don't have at least five minutes a day to nurture my soul and refresh my mind."

Now, what are the rewards for taking five? You'll discover an amazing sense of clarity in your thinking. You'll begin to see your life in a different perspective. You'll realize you're in the presence of the Almighty, and you'll discover your problems aren't so big after all.

Take five minutes a day, friend. It'll be the best five of your day.

Dear God,
help me to be a faithful steward of Your time.
Amen.

[Elisha] picked up the cloak that had fallen from Elijah and went back and stood on the bank of the Jordan. Then he took the cloak...and struck the water with it...When he struck the water, it divided...and he crossed over...the prophets from Jericho, who were watching, said, "The spirit of Elijah is resting on Elisha."

2 Kings 2:13–15, NIV

Mantles and Mentors

Brad Sargent

Isn't it amazing how a chance relationship can have a lasting impact? That's what happened when I introduced myself to Bob Winter at a seminar on Christian ministry to people affected by AIDS.

For two years, God had been nudging me to get involved with this issue that many Christians had avoided. I pleaded, "But this doesn't make sense, Lord. I don't even know a single person with AIDS!" However, when I saw the notice for the seminar, I knew I was supposed to attend. And Bob was the first person with AIDS I'd ever met.

Bob shared the many spiritual lessons the Lord had taught him through suffering with AIDS. And he communicated a desire to minister by giving the good news and hope to others infected with the HIV virus. He was exhausted from constantly battling nausea and a fever exceeding one hundred degrees. It was a risk for him to be there, since he was vulnerable to catching an illness from other conferees.

The Lord used Bob and the rest of the seminar to touch me in a profound way. Subsequently, I attended other conferences that summer including an AIDS ministry training session in August that Bob also attended. Extremely ill, he had to go home prematurely. It was the last time I saw him—he died in December—but it was not the end of his impact on my life and my AIDS ministry.

It was as if Bob's mantle fell upon me. As with Elisha, the "waters parted" and eight months after meeting Bob, I found myself as secretary on the executive committee for a national coalition of churches and ministries dedicated to helping people affected by AIDS! Imagine my wonderment when several months later, a mutual friend sent a letter Bob wrote in 1988 outlining his vision of just such a coalition. I'd been helping implement his outline almost point for point, before I even knew what that outline was. Now it delights me to pass along the vision for AIDS ministry to others.

Do you have a mantle to pass, a vision, or skills, or wisdom that you can risk sharing with those who you are, or could be, mentoring?

Father God,
what awesome gifts You give us in Your providence!
Help me pass along my mantles to others.
Amen.

These [trials] have come so that your faith—
of greater worth than gold,
which perishes even though refined by fire—
may be proved genuine and may result in
praise, glory, and honor when Jesus Christ is revealed.

1 Peter 1: 7, NIV

I'd Wished I'd Been Fired

Giles Scott

I've been a service manager with a copier company for five and a half years. For the first four years, things went well. I got good reviews and I could do little wrong.

But then, one by one, things began to happen. First, there were several unfortunate errors that cost the company money. The owners decided that some of these errors were my fault (and not unrightly so), and I began to experience the beginning of their displeasure with my performance.

Second, in the last six months, we decided to merge another department with the copier department. In the process, two positions were eliminated. Within three months, three of my best technicians decided to change careers. Another decided to move out of the area. The net result: I was faced with having to make the same amount of customers happy with two-thirds of the manpower needed.

All of a sudden, customers were waiting for service too long. That, combined with the owner's previous year's displeasure, put my job in great jeopardy. This, plus attempting to do approximately three jobs at once, put me under great stress.

It all culminated one Friday evening when one of the owners came to me and vented his frustration. No matter what I said or did, I couldn't make him happy. The service department was in shambles. The shop was totally unorganized. Customers weren't being taken care of in a timely fashion.

I prayed all weekend, "Lord, what can I do? I'm only one person. I can't do it all." And, finally, "Lord, I know You won't let me quit, but I wouldn't mind if You got me fired."

There was nothing else I could do but submit my future to the Lord. I had thought I had done that in the past, but I truly hadn't. There was still some of me involved. The Lord showed me that I was trying to make others happy in my work rather than Him. And He showed me that the work I did was out of a need for income and personal fulfillment, not out of a desire to be a servant. At that moment, the Holy Spirit granted me a gift. He gave me the desire to serve the owners and my fellow employees. But most of all, He gave me a gladness of spirit for the difficulties that were occurring.

Father,
I thank You for trials.
I thank You for how You use people and difficult situations
to draw me to a place where all I want to do is serve You
and bring glory to Your name.
I know I haven't always handled adversity perfectly,
but I also know that through my weaknesses,
I am made strong in You.
Amen.

The Lord said, "If I find fifty righteous people in the city of Sodom, I will spare the whole place for their sake."

Genesis 18:26, NIV

A Few Good Men

Robert C. Smith

As a young, black, poverty-stricken kid growing up in a small town in Louisiana, one of my greatest ambitions was to leave the plantation as soon as I finished high school, or sooner if the opportunity presented itself.

On the plantation where I lived, cotton was king, and the Boss and Boll Weevil were the only beings I knew that loved the crop. I hated it.

Oftentimes, my family and I picked cotton from "can't see in the morning to can't see at night."

I remember the hot midday sun that caused me to search for shade as I waited with sweat dripping from my face until the water-boy came to bring the ice-water to quench my thirst.

Cotton and sun dominated my life. And it seemed as if the more I worked, the less I had. So at eighteen years of age, I concluded the only way out, the only way to get ahead, was to join the United States Marine Corps. I'd seen a sign that read, "The Marines are looking for a few good men." Also on that sign was a man dressed in a red, white, and blue uniform. I immediately fell in love with it. I joined the Corps to get off the plantation and into one of those beautiful uniforms.

However, I knew little about the high price I would pay to become one of the few good men, and wear that dress-blue uniform. After thirteen weeks of rough and rugged boot-camp, then four years of daily training, and a tour in Vietnam, I was not so sure anymore that I wanted to be one of "the few, the proud, and the brave." It was after leaving the Corps that I realized more than ever that I was already part of another group of fighting men.

You see, God, too, is looking for *a few good men,* but as I learned in the Corps—just as it is in God's army—there is a high price to pay if a man determines to live righteously for God in an unrighteous world.

No matter where you work, no matter how you earn your living, are you willing to pay the price in order to become one of God's few good men?

Lord,
thank You for the great opportunities that You give me.
Continue to challenge me to become
one of the few good men You are looking for.
Amen.

There is no wisdom, no insight, no plan
that can succeed against the Lord.
The horse is made ready for the day of battle,
but victory rests with the Lord.

Proverbs 21:30–31, NIV

Battle Ready

John Strubhar

Men, when we choose to be on God's side, we'll be at war with three enemies: the world, the flesh, and the devil!

The "world" is society apart from God. It includes a value system that ignores God and scoffs at the idea of His presence in human life. The "flesh" is the sin nature we inherited from Adam. The "devil" is the power source behind the value system ignoring God. When we earnestly endeavor to please God, we'll constantly be in combat with the enemy.

"But hold on," you say, "how can this be? I'm involved in my church. I maintain balance in my life. I strive to make a difference for God!" There's the reason, my friend. If you're trying to please the Lord, you'll find yourself in perpetual battle between your *calling*, namely your family relationships, and your ministry, which is your work or vocational assignment. Let me explain.

As men, our primary source of personal fulfillment is our job or our ministry, which helps us provide for our family, make a living, and gain the respect of our peers. However, when ministry takes precedence over calling, our family life deteriorates. We may still live under the same roof, but there isn't the intimacy and sense of expectancy we once enjoyed. When this occurs, the enemy has stuck his foot in the door of our home. Unless we provide a proactive leadership of love, the results will be devastating. Relationships that we value most will erode. Unconsciously, we may begin to compensate by spending even more time in our ministry. The workplace, however, is no haven for safety and security.

To the contrary, the workplace naturally tears at our spiritual fiber. Stress in our ministry is compounded when our calling is out of whack. Instead of looking forward to coming home, we dread it. We can't handle another conflict or solve another problem. We retreat behind newspapers or fall asleep watching television. The enemy scores another victory!

We need to be wise to the enemy's strategy. We can do this by prioritizing our calling, intentionally writing spouses and children into our daily schedules, and by saying no to outside interests so we can say yes to our family's needs. We seize the reins of leadership in our calling, directing our families toward God. And we encourage our peers to hold us accountable for our performance in both our calling and our ministry.

As our calling is prioritized, our ministry will become even more fulfilling. We'll have new energy to meet the demands made upon us. Because we're balancing our calling and ministry, we'll slam the door on Satan's attempts to destroy God's mighty work in our lives. How great it is to know that the Lord Jesus, through His death and resurrection, overcame the world, the flesh, and the devil. Men, as we become battle-ready, Christ's victory will become ours as well!

Lord Jesus,
help me to become more like You. May You empower me to manage
my life so that Satan cannot destroy my calling or my ministry.
Thank You for Your overcoming power, that is mine today.
Amen.

It is finished.

John 19:30, NIV

It's Done!

Paul P. Tell, Jr.

"How are you coming on that?" my father asked.

"It's done," I replied with a smile. It felt good to show him the new twenty-page lease I'd prepared. It was ready to go.

Something good had emerged from my desk, which was covered with files and piles of redrafted copies scribbled with notes. The finished product looked so simple now, almost beautiful in its neatness and order. Sometimes, it seems, the better the job, the harder it is for me to understand the reason for clutter and why it took so long to complete.

Next time it'll be easier, I muse. But it never is.

As I read the words of Jesus, "It is finished," I think of the awful pressure and agony He was experiencing. There is beauty and victory in His completion. It extends far beyond my understanding. Though I can't comprehend it fully, I know He finished the greatest work of all.

His example and words send a challenge to keep working and finish what He began in us when we came to faith in Him. It seems so easy to neglect the really important things that build our character, bring us spiritual power, and reveal Christ in us to others. Why is it so easy to be distracted and do what is less important? Maybe it's like my preparation of that real estate lease. It's an involved and messy process at times, and it takes steady work. Often it seems easier to put off the bigger projects and decisions and let them wait a little longer while I get smaller and easier tasks out of the way. I'm so glad Jesus didn't think like this.

I find my backlog of work never really clearing, but I know I must be diligent about the work He has for me. I know, too, that of all of my activities, those things I do for my family and others are what pleases and honors God.

Lord Jesus,
You finished Your work, and I know You want me to finish, too.
I need Your help to put the things around me in order,
and, most of all,
I need Your help to put myself in order.
Amen.

Each man has his own gift from God.

1 Corinthians 7:7, NASB

I've Always Wanted to Be a Runner

Richie G. Thomas

While serving as a pastor in Lawrence, Kansas—the home of the University of Kansas—I had the opportunity to attend several national track events. The Kansas Relays are the school's premier event each year, and it attracts athletes from all over the world.

I was always amazed by the physical diversity of the athletes from event to event: runners (dash, middle, and long distance), jumpers (pole vaulters, broad jumpers, hurdlers, and high jumpers), and throwers (discus, javelin, hammer, and shot-putters).

Men and women who were superstars in their specialty event would not, and probably could not, even be competitive in other events. For instance, I watched records being set in the shot put by men who built muscle mass and developed techniques that would only embarrass them if they decided to compete in the high jump. As I watched a half-dozen events taking place on the same field, I caught a new vision of the church.

Our diversity, which is often the source of controversy, is not our weakness but our strength. Each member of the body is wonderfully gifted by a common Giver but unique by the design of that common Giver. God has made each of us peculiar. Our peculiarity makes the individual vital to the whole. I'm made, I'm gifted, and I'm conditioned for my event.

God never intended for any man to be a complete, comprehensive package, able to do everything. He said at the beginning, "It is not good for man to be alone." God has made lifters of loads. God has made speedy messengers. God has also made runners, throwers, and jumpers. Each in his pursuit of excellence is a servant to the will of God.

Father,
give me the wisdom to know my gift.
Give me the courage to excel.
Give me the grace to appreciate and not be envious or critical
of others and their gifts.
Amen.

Whatever you do, work at it with all your heart,
as working for the Lord, not for men,
since you know that you will receive an inheritance from the Lord
as a reward.

Colossians 3:23–24, NIV

Response—Ability

Ray C. Veal

You've probably had similar experiences to the one I am about to share. I suppose we could call them lessons we learn—or should learn—as we tread along our mortal paths. I've had memorable incidents throughout my life that seem to "stick" with me; I call them my "Velcro memories." They're not really that profound, but rather like life's little cue cards that pop up at the most appropriate times.

A dozen or so years ago, as I was hurrying through several unoccupied rooms in one of the campus buildings where I worked, I walked past a small, but noticeable, organic-looking mess on the floor. In the next space of a second I had what seemed like at least a ten-minute conversation with myself.

Before I had taken two full steps past that mess, I heard a still small voice ask me, "Is that your response—ability?" That brief hesitation in pronouncing the syllables of the word *responsibility* spoke volumes to me about whether or not I had developed the Christ-like ability to respond from the heart to certain situations. In this mental conversation, I halfheartedly offered myself a few lame excuses, such as, "We have a janitorial crew to do this sort of cleaning," and "I'm in a hurry to get back to my office; it's not my job!" No fellow employees would have known that I had been in the room that day, but I knew that I knew—and He knew, too. So, in what seemed like a lifetime, but was only a few seconds, a deep impression was made on me about why we do the things we do. And why I do the things I do.

After those couple of steps, I stopped sharply, went to the janitorial closet, found a rag, and proceeded to clean up the mess. Now you don't necessarily have to be a Christian to do a good deed. But I am continually being taught that as I grow to be more like Him, and as I allow Him to grow in me, I am therefore growing in the ability to respond as He would.

I responded, not because my deed would have been seen by men, or even because I could pat myself on the back. Neither the pride of life nor the praise of man can ever replace the heavenly reward in the words, "Well done, good and faithful servant."

Lord,
thank You for reminding me that I should labor,
not to be seen by men or only to please men,
but as Your servant in all areas of my life,
at work, at home, and in the community.
Grant me the ability to respond as You would in all situations.
Amen.

Since you are my rock and my fortress,
for the sake of your name
lead and guide me.

Psalm 31:3, NIV

Take It to the Bank

Dennis E. Way

For many weeks I searched for a car. Not just any car, it had to be a two-door convertible. A real sporty model. It also had to have low mileage and be within a certain price range.

I'm a used car dealer and I specialize in providing vehicles on request. Twice each week I start out at 5:30 in the morning and, within a radius of over one hundred miles from home, drive to wholesale auto auctions. I prowl long lines of cars like a detective, trying to match the needs of clients with what's there to be auctioned. I even go to dealers in other cities in search of just the right vehicle. I don't hesitate to pass by cars that aren't what I'm looking for. If I see flaws or potential problems that my customers might not notice, I keep on looking for just the right car.

In this case, after three months of searching, the right car was finally found. I called long-distance to my customer who said yes, the glistening turquoise color was good. The mileage was exceptionally low and the price was just a little more than the limit we'd discussed, but it was still much less than the market had been bringing for this make and model.

My customer also said yes to the purchase, so I paid out nearly ten thousand dollars and brought the car home, satisfied my customer was being well served. I was looking forward to closing the transaction the next morning, but by then everything changed.

For reasons I was unable to discern, my customer expressed a definite change of mind from less than twenty-four hours before, completely denying our telephone conversation, which clearly communicated an approval of both the color and the price. I was shocked.

What was at stake was more than money, although that's just as important to me as it is to every other breadwinner and small business person. What was at stake was trust, faith, and integrity—mine. What was also at stake was my willingness to put myself, my family, and my business financially at risk based on someone else's intentions. The purchase had been made from my own bank account and I didn't need the car sitting on my lot waiting for another customer to materialize.

More fundamentally, what was at stake was my faith in God, and I'm pleased to say it never wavered. Now, you might be wondering how God got into the middle of an automobile transaction, so I have to tell you that I try to involve Him in everything I do, especially in my business. Sometimes I forget. But I always know how valuable my connection with Him is in every aspect of my life.

While my trust in human beings got another reasonable jolt of caution, this experience reinforced that my one and only, absolutely certain object of trust is God. If I need to sharpen my skills for measuring customer sincerity, I know I don't have to question what God intends. He doesn't let me down. He doesn't lead me astray. His dependability is rock solid. And I can take that to the bank every day, for sure.

Lord,

help me to walk in faithfulness and integrity,
and to be led by Your will and not my own.
Amen.

But someone may well say,
"You have faith, and I have works;
show me your faith without the works,
and I will show you my faith by my works.

James 2:18, NASB

Words Only Whisper

Donald E. White

The afternoon discussion was not going well at our Bible camp in Alaska. The topic was setting and attaining goals. We were discussing an old adage, "The will to win is worthless without the will to prepare." It was obvious, however, that their thoughts were not on the discussion, but on the next event, the camp's annual two-mile race. Life returned to the group when we dismissed and began preparing for that activity.

There was excitement and talking at the starting line, as campers predicted the winner. Good athletes stimulated more rivalry by proclaiming themselves the obvious winner.

Arnie, an Eskimo teenager from Nome, leaned against a big cottonwood tree, waiting for the race to start. He was a quiet, likable young man, but I had not heard of his athletic ability. I asked Arnie if he was a good runner, but he only indicated that he did like to run. He told me his family spent the summer at their fishing cabin a few miles down the beach from Nome and he regularly ran to town for supplies or to see friends.

The starting signal sounded and the race began. Arnie moved out quickly and set a fast pace for a two-mile run. One runner yelled, "Arnie, Arnie, slow down or you'll burn out." It seemed Arnie didn't hear, as he continued running intently.

The staff and other campers soon moved to the finish line where we would wait for the winner. Straining to see who was coming around the last turn, we couldn't believe our eyes. It was Arnie! He didn't slow down and he didn't burn out! He ran smoothly right across the finish line, far ahead of the others. His running silenced all predictions.

Determination, hard work, ability, and love for running had allowed Arnie to win the annual race. He had accomplished what others could only talk about.

Later, our discussion group compared the race to endeavors in life. We learned that faith, words, goals, and dreams mean little, unless they result in positive actions. Interestingly, those kids are now grown and some have achieved leadership in business, education, and the Christian ministry. They dreamed, they worked, and they won. I pray they'll always remember there is another race tomorrow.

Dear Lord Jesus,
I thank You for the hope You have given me
and the faith that I can do all things through You.
Help me, Lord, to prepare, to work,
and to continue to reach goals in my life.
Amen.

Now faith is the substance of things hoped for,
the evidence of things not seen.

Hebrews 11:1, KJV

The Race of Life

Gene Wilder

What is faith? Like so many words that deal with abstracts, it's difficult to define. Oh, yes, the biblical definition is superb: "Faith is the substance of things hoped for, the evidence of things not seen." But again, what is faith? A few years ago, while I was trying to describe faith to a group of fifth graders, one of the pupils gave me a new definition.

Innocently, the young scholar began, "Preacher, I know this might not sound right, but I think faith is what you have when you go to the track. You see, faith is what you have when you put your money on a horse and believe that horse will win. Faith is picking a winner and putting your money on him."

Obviously, this young theologian's definition of faith cannot be found in the eleventh chapter of Hebrews, or anywhere else in the Bible, but despite its earthiness, my young friend's view of faith was profoundly accurate.

Faith is putting your bet on the one you believe will win. For the Christian, faith is putting your money, as well as everything else, on

Christ, believing that when the race of life is over, Christ will be the winner.

Not all who wear the name "Christian" are possessors of such faith. Some have placed their bets on less favored runners. Some have their bets riding on the filly of financial success. Others have placed their bets on the horse of popularity. Others hope the horse of career achievement will bring home the winning purse. But those who have faith in Jesus Christ *spend it all* on no other runner but Him. Faith is an all-or-nothing bet placed on belief in a victorious Christ.

So it's off to the races, that is, the race of life. The horses are lined up and ready to run. Only one will win when the race is done. The starter announces, "Ladies and gentlemen, place your bets."

My bet's on Christ. How are you betting?

Dear Lord,
help me today to run the race of life
with all that I am and all that I have,
totally entrusted to Your loving care.
In Jesus' name I pray.
Amen.

In everything,
do to others what you would have them do to you,
for this sums up the Law and the Prophets.

Matthew 7:12, NIV

Can a Christian Be a Salesman?

Dick Williams

I had been a Christian for three years, gone to Bible school, and was now faced with the need to find a job to support my wife, Karen, and our four kids. As I prayed for direction, it seems our Lord was telling me to go back into sales. I thought, *No way!*

Before I was a Christian I had sold encyclopedias and building materials. My driving motivation had been to make money. Now that I was a Christian, I knew that money should not be the focus of my life. So how could the Lord want me to go back into sales and do something I thought was contrary to His ways? Needless to say, I lost the argument with God and finally took a job selling for a steel company.

As I was learning my product line, I began to call on potential customers. At first it was slow going because not only did it take time to build trust and confidence with customers, but also I was struggling to understand how God could be at the center of my life when I was selling. Without money to motivate me, what would keep me going when the sales were not coming in as fast as my boss thought they should?

Slowly I began to realize that by becoming genuinely interested in the needs of my customers and by serving them, I could represent our Lord in a way that pleased Him. The more I found creative ways to serve my customers, the more my sales increased. Making money was no longer my focus, however; serving my customers was.

As time passed, I built relationships with my customers. Some of them shared personal needs, as well as trials they were facing. This gave me an opportunity to encourage them and pray with some of them.

How thankful I am today that I learned how to be a Christian in the marketplace. Now as a pastor I can encourage other brothers in Christ that they can be successful by doing unto others what they would have others do unto them.

Father,
I pray that You will help me pass on to others
the lessons I have learned—
that it is possible to live out my Christian convictions in my jobs
and that developing the heart of a servant is what You desire.
Truly, if I seek to serve others, You will take care of my needs.
Amen.

Blessed be the Lord, who daily bears our burden, the God who is our salvation. God is to us a God of deliverances.

Psalm 68:19–20, NASB

Keep Me from Being Crushed

James E. Bolton

As I was walking back from the grocery store, I went under a railroad overpass just as a freight train started across it. First, I heard the engines as they strained to pull dozens of freight cars. Next, I heard the creaks and groans of the bridge girders bearing the weight of the heavy train.

While this was happening, I realized that the wood and steel girders were all that was keeping me from being crushed by the train. Yet I was walking freely underneath because the girders were bearing the heavy load.

"That's how I bear your burdens. I keep you from being crushed by them," I felt Jesus saying to me.

I prayed, "Lord, I feel that I'm being crushed by the burdens of unemployment and not having enough money to buy food and pay my many bills. Somehow, Lord, can You take the burden and provide the money that I need as You've done in the past?"

And under that trestle, in the midst of my personal turmoil, I felt the comforting presence of Jesus telling me that He would provide for my needs. There and then, He revealed to me how to get some money both through working for friends and contacting social relief programs.

I felt the Lord lifting my burdens and giving me peace of mind. I was protected.

Thank You, Lord Jesus,
for bearing my burdens so that I won't be crushed by them.
Amen.

God has told us his secret reason for sending Christ,
a plan he decided on in mercy long ago;
and this was his purpose: that when the time is ripe
he will gather us all together from wherever we are—
in heaven or on earth—to be with him in Christ, forever.

Ephesians 1:9–10, TLB

The Weekend Report

Charles R. Brown

For many, the five o'clock whistle is a signal for celebration. "Let the games begin!" In some offices, employees could get whiplash from the suction created as all the doors open outward at the same time. The parking lot is a blur as people race from the workplace.

For the Monday-through-Friday worker, the two days off slip by much too quickly. Coworkers are greeted with a puffy-eyed, "Goo' morning," some taking longer than others to accept the reality that this really is Monday, this is the office, and the boss does expect some work to be done at least until closing time. Conversations around the coffee machine, for those awake enough at least, usually find someone asking about the past two days.

"How was your weekend?"

"Oh, let's see...Saturday night we went to the Billy Bo Bob concert at the amphitheater. It was fantastic!"

Or, "Aw, we didn't do nothin' much. Worked in the yard a little and watched some TV."

Perhaps someone will offer, "My wife spent most of Saturday evening and all of Sunday in the emergency room with our youngest. Mikie managed to fall from his tree house and broke his arm. What did you do this weekend?"

"I went to church," I answer.

"Oh, yeah. Want some more coffee? Hey, did you see the game Sunday afternoon?"

My opportunity to share didn't get my best response. Often it seems I have difficulty communicating the joy that comes from the time of worship and fellowship, generally the highlight of the last two days. Maybe my weekend report should be a little more enthusiastic, even understated just to get my listener's attention.

"Naw, didn't do much. Jus' went to church, encountered the God of the universe and beyond, visited with some of the most wonderful people I know, and then went home and had lunch."

I hope I can live as some other Christians have: "Every day, in places of worship and in home fellowship groups, they were faithful in teaching and telling the good news that Jesus is the Christ—the Messiah" (Acts 5:42, author paraphrase).

Thank You, Father,
for the fellowship with other believers
and the opportunity to worship together.
Let this time of worship spill over into the entire week,
and grant me freedom to share the secret.
Amen.

"For My thoughts are not your thoughts,
neither are your ways My ways," declares the Lord.
"For as the heavens are higher than the earth,
so are My ways higher than your ways,
and My thoughts than your thoughts."

Isaiah 55:8–9, NASB

Go Ahead, Ruin My Day

Jerry R. Carr

I answered the phone at work, giving my caller a cheerful greeting, wishing her a good morning. But as we proceeded with our conversation it was obvious that this Good Sam was not a happy camper, and the fact that I seemed to be having a great day did not help the matter one iota. Finally, unable to stand the whole air of our conversation, she burst out, "I hate to pop your bubble, but I've called to ruin your day!" With that, she proceeded to unload, with great precision and eloquence, a detailed description of how I was responsible for one of the greatest processing blunders of the century.

As I mentally picked myself up from the floor, I was filled with a wide array of emotions, and my mind whirled with thoughts, not all positive, edifying, or godly. Then somewhere beyond my thoughts and emotions came a still small voice that said, "No one can ruin the day of a child of God." Remembering the counsel of Proverbs 15:1, that "A soft answer turns away wrath, but a harsh word stirs up anger," I decided to forsake my witty (or was it witless?) come-back and go the way of the

Word of God. I responded, "So, how can I help you resolve this problem?" In a few moments her anger had subsided, we were working on solutions, and, much to my amazement, my angry caller began to speak to me as though we were the dearest of friends.

As I hung up the phone, I was overwhelmed by a sense of awe in God's wisdom and counsel, and thought to myself, *You know, this stuff really works.* I whispered, "Thank You, Lord," and went on with my daily duties.

Lord,
how majestic are Your ways,
how marvelous Your counsel.
You are the all-wise God,
the God of wisdom, counsel, and understanding.
Teach me today and everyday the wisdom of forsaking my way
and my wisdom to yielding to Yours.
Amen.

"For I know the plans that I have for you,"
declares the Lord,
"plans for welfare and not for calamity
to give you a future and a hope."

Jeremiah 29:11, NASB

New Hope

Bernard Epperson

My life was a shambles. The factory, where I had an excellent job, had closed, and my wife had left me. My heart felt shattered. Everything I worked so hard for seemed ruined.

People whispered I was finished, that my life was over. I wondered if they were right. I prayed hard for the Lord to rebuild my life and give me a new start. Eventually I found another job, but it was at the very bottom of the company, at very little money. It would take me years to work my way back up to where I was on my old job. My wife knew that and would have nothing to do with me.

About this time, the church I attend had a weekend retreat for men planned at a remote camp. I didn't have a penny to spare, but someone paid my way and encouraged me to go. I prayed, and it seemed God wanted me to go. So I did.

As I mingled with the others and I heard them talk about their families and good jobs, I wondered how my life would end up. Did God have a purpose for me? Was my life ruined, or would things work out?

On Saturday afternoon, between study and prayer sessions, we all gathered in the gym to play basketball. As the ball bounced out of bounds one man jumped for it. He crashed through a window and cut his arm badly. Blood spurted from the wound, and quickly he went into shock.

Most of the other men panicked. But I had received Red Cross first aid training, so I stayed calm and took charge, covering the wound with my handkerchief and using pressure to stop the bleeding. Someone wanted to apply a tourniquet, but I knew that was used only when there is a choice between a life or a limb, and I felt that the arm would be saved. I bandaged the wound and saw that the man got to the hospital, where his arm was saved and he recovered fully. He serves the Lord today.

As the victim left for the hospital, I noticed that both of my hands were covered with blood. It was a vivid reminder for me. That evening I knelt and thanked God for using me. My life wasn't ruined. Through His leading I was still a useful part of His kingdom.

Lord,

I thank You that whatever trials I go through,

You can always rebuild me and bring me on to better things.

Amen.

Some Pharisees saw this and asked his disciples,
"Why does your teacher eat with such people?" Jesus heard them and
answered, "People who are well do not need a doctor, but only those
who are sick. Go and find out what is meant by the scripture that
says: 'It is kindness that I want, not animal sacrifices.' I have not
come to call respectable people, but outcasts."

Matthew 9:11–13, TEV

A View from the Fortieth Floor

James H. Harrison

It's called "The Financial District." Residing here are banks from every corner of the world, corporate offices of multinational businesses, and law firms so large they extend to eight and ten floors of a fifty-five story building. The furnishings in the offices of these institutions are plush. Rare paintings, tapestries, and period furniture adorn the waiting rooms and conference halls.

Employees move about quietly, nearly unnoticed. They are dutifully busy with designated tasks. I don't recognize any evidence of feelings for accomplishment or fulfillment or satisfaction. The reward for many of them is a simple paycheck.

You see, I work in one of these offices, on the fortieth floor. I'm acquainted with many of these people. I see them come and go. Occasionally we even get to know something personal about one another. On even rarer occasions we exchange our faith journey and witness the Living Christ in our lives. Most of the time, though, it's difficult to see Jesus on the fortieth floor. I don't feel fulfilled here.

Outside, forty floors down, the homeless move about in the noise and bustle of the city. They rummage and live day by day. Their reward is a single meal and a dry place to sleep in one of the city parks they call home. It's here that I actually found a community of Jesus.

Amongst the homeless there's a small group that read Scripture, study the Word, and share their food and tools. They talk and listen to each other with genuine care and love. It's odd how this congregation draws me. I find Jesus here much easier than on the fortieth floor. Jesus lives here. He's present within this small band of people, networking in the camp of the oppressed.

I'm so moved by the witness of the living Christ here that I've asked if I could join their Bible study. They accept even me. I am at home.

Dear God,
with Your grace You kindly invite me into discipleship with Jesus.
Help me witness the living faith of the One who knows the way.
In His name I pray.
Amen.

Put on…humility…forgiving each other.

Colossians 3:12–13, NASB

Forgiveness at Work

C. S. McMinn

My stomach squirmed as an all-too-familiar truck skidded into our driveway. The driver leaped out and stooped to pick up some sheet metal lying on the ground.

"Hey! What do you think you're doing?" I yelled. He paused, looking toward me. "The boss sent me over," he replied, his voice indifferent, matter-of-fact.

Something snapped inside me. "You tell Jack no one comes here without permission. So, get out, now!" He froze, his face stunned. Without another word he drove off. I took three huge breaths. The previous owner of this property, "the boss," had been very difficult to deal with.

Within minutes, the truck returned—fast. Before Jack's feet hit the dirt, he started yelling, "Who do you think you are, you jerk! That's my metal! How dare you stop my men?"

I hollered back, "You owe me for storing this junk! It's been here six months and you have to ask before you send out your gorilla."

"Owe you?" His face purpled, eyes bulging. "Owe you?" For a second I thought he was going to hit me. His fists shook with fury and cuss words boiled from his lips, "OWE YOU?" he screamed. Hatred blazed between us. "You wait," he snarled. "My attorney will rip you to pieces. That's my metal and you'll rot in hell before you get a penny." Then he spun on his heel, gunned the engine, and tore off in a shower of gravel.

We were both contractors; the thought of seeing him again, either at the lumberyard or around town, was unbearable. So, hours later, I prayed, "Lord, what do I do?" For once, the Lord's voice was clear: *Phone him up and apologize.*

"What?" I blustered, "APOLOGIZE?"

Yes, said the Lord, *ask for his forgiveness.*

"But, Lord," I pleaded, "he was wrong!" *And so were you,* the Lord replied. And my pride began to crumble...

Finally, late that night, I phoned. "Is Jack there?" I stammered. A familiar voice came on the line. "I'm calling to apologize for my behavior today," I blurted. "You can pick up your sheet metal."

Silence.

Finally, in a voice of total shock and disbelief, Jack whispered, "Well...I'm sorry, too. And you can have that metal. I don't need it. Thank you."

We did meet later, at the lumberyard. He was polite, subdued, baffled even. Something powerful had gone on between us, something born out of desperate prayer and completed by obedience.

Lord,

show me how obedient humility releases Your power

upon those with whom I work.

Amen.

Then, because so many people were coming and going that they did not even have a chance to eat, he said to them, "Come with me by yourselves to a quiet place and get some rest." So they went away by themselves in a boat to a solitary place. But many who saw them leaving recognized them and ran on foot from all the towns and got there ahead of them.

Mark 6:31–33, NIV

Take a Break

Louis Merryman

Jesus wanted to take His busy disciples on vacation. They were in need of time away. They needed rest. They needed proper nourishment. They needed to share with each other all they'd done and taught. None of these needs could be met in the hustle and bustle of their everyday routine.

So Jesus and the disciples climbed aboard a boat for a peaceful journey to a quiet location. Their destination was to be a solitary place away from inhabited places. A great place for a vacation. Unfortunately, their solitude lasted only for the time they were on the boat. Jesus' fans knew where He was going and got there first. Once Jesus and the disciples touched solid ground their vacation was over.

One of my grown sons and I went on vacation in Utah. We ate well. We caught up on family stuff, especially his. We did men stuff: hiking, golfing, and rafting. One morning we slept late, and another morning we got up early and went hot air ballooning.

Soon after the balloon lifted off, my fears vanished. The mountains were magnificent in the light of the early dawn. The sun kissed us. We smiled at the ant-people who scurried below us in matchbox cars. For the brief time we were in the air I felt the deep solitude I think Jesus and His disciples sought. Except for the occasional blast of the balloon's jumbo burner, the only sound was the soft singing of the morning breezes.

As nice as that flight was for us, I realized we don't have to go hot air ballooning to find solitude. Getaways are important, but their location can be found much nearer at hand.

Today, we can find a place of solitude, and take a break, by resting in God's love and grace, and soaring above the problems of the day.

Thank You, Father,
for Jesus' concern about His disciples' well-being.
Help me to follow His example and find those times and places
where I may rest with You and with those I love.
Amen.

Therefore if any man is in Christ, he is a new creature; the old things passed away; behold, new things have come.

2 Corinthians 5:17, NASB

Rejected or Renewed?

Al Munger

We anchored and rowed ashore in the dinghy to explore one of the Gulf Islands in British Columbia. It was a warm morning and we could smell the field grass drying in the sun.

My wife, Erika, was first to notice the sign: "Pottery."

Up the road we found the potter's shack, a split-shake building, with one room for display and sales and a back room where the potter sat at his wheel. Clay and water were at his side. We watched as he molded the clay with his hands, occasionally wetting them to keep the clay soft. It was fascinating, and the finished pot held great promise of being a thing of beauty when it was fired and the colors would appear.

I noticed the back door of the potter's shack was open. Behind the shack was a large pile of broken pottery. Vessels that did not turn out well were destined to go there. The potter had simply tossed them on the scrap pile.

That scene reminded me of God's message to Jeremiah, "Go down to the potter's house" (Jer. 18:2). Jeremiah went. Here was the potter at work; but as he watched, "The vessel that he was making of clay was spoiled in the hand of the potter." Did he toss it on the scrap heap? Did the potter start over with new clay? As Jeremiah watched, "He remade it into another vessel, as it pleased the potter to make" (Jer. 18:4).

Remade, not rejected! What great news for any man who's made mistakes, for the man who knows disappointments, for the fellow who thinks he's blown it. God takes the same clay and forms it into a new vessel of honor and service. We aren't tossed on the pile of broken dreams. We aren't consigned to the dump. The Master Potter puts our clay on the wheel once again. There is a new beginning, a new man, fashioned from the same clay, as we yield to the Potter's hand.

There is a great difference between "all things new" and "all new things." In a culture like ours that is so familiar with the disposable, the throw-aways of everyday life, it's wonderfully reassuring to know that Jesus has a better plan to deal with imperfection. He will use the same clay, remove the twigs and stones, and build a better man.

Jesus,
thank You for being so patient with me,
for purifying and molding this clay into the kind of man
my wife and family can live with and love,
a man remade, not rejected.
Amen.

I do not understand what I do.
For what I want to do I do not do, but what I hate I do.
And if I do what I do not want to do,
I agree that the law is good.
As it is, it is no longer I myself who do it, but it is sin living in me.

Romans 7:15–17, NIV

Life on a Gridlocked Freeway

Eric M. Nishimoto

It's always dark when I get home from work, and I'm always tired from working too hard, and numb from driving too long. Excessive overtime and endless lines of crawling bumper-to-bumper freeway traffic always drain my energy and humor. It seems the best paying jobs are in the city, far away from our quiet and serene suburban home. So I make this commuting trip six days a week. Without good money and a good home I wouldn't feel as if I were keeping my family as happy and healthy as I should.

I really love my wife and sons, but you wouldn't know it by the way I act toward them when I finally get home from work. By then even my dear family becomes nothing more than a major irritant.

You'd think my sons were little Machiavellian imps by the way I yell and send them to their rooms. And you might suspect my wife was a thorny shrew by the way I treat her. Though my heart yearns for time with the family, my flesh allows for very little. Much of our time together is unhappy, angry, and downright miserable.

I'm in a constant state of bewilderment. I know and want what's good, or at least seems right. Unfortunately, my more expansive heart and soul is confined in flesh that is severely restricted and regularly challenged. Consequently, I seem to be unhappy most of the time. My spiritual dissonance stays strong because my physical self is unable to keep up with the demands of my conscience, especially with a flesh that caves in to the pressures and diversions of a materially comfortable life.

As weak and corrupted as my own efforts are, you'd think that I'd stop relying on myself to consistently do what's good. Maybe it's time for me to drop the inadequate direction of my body and tap into the God-given power of the Holy Spirit. What a novel idea. It's so simple that I tend to overlook it. Every day.

Lord,
my world beats my flesh constantly.
I'm too frail to be the husband and father I should.
Thank You for the power of Your Holy Spirit
to overcome the entropy I allow this world to create in me.
Amen.

You are old, and your sons do not walk in your ways.

1 Samuel 8:5, NIV

Winning My Children

Giles Scott

I had just changed jobs. Actually, I had more than changed jobs; I had changed vocations, from a technical career to sales. I had made this change for the best of reasons—to provide for my growing family.

My wife and I had been married for a little over two years, and we already had two children; the first within thirteen months after our wedding, and the second, thirteen months after the first. So, naturally, I was feeling the pressure of providing an adequate living. Additionally, we were living in an area of California where the cost of living had far outstripped the wages. The only way to increase my earning potential seemed to be in sales.

So there I was; if I didn't produce sales, I wouldn't be paid. In order to produce the required sales to feed my family, I felt compelled to be in front of my customers eight hours a day, which left only the evenings for proposal preparation and organization. Needless to say, there was precious little time left over for my wife and two young sons. It seemed the attention I did give my children occurred when they attracted it, which was mostly in a negative fashion. Of course, I responded mostly in a negative fashion.

Then, one day, in a rather good mood—I must have just closed a deal—I called to my oldest son, who was eighteen months old at the time, "Come here, Jonathan. Sit on my lap and let me read you a story." His answer: "No, I want Mommy!" And he ran to his mother.

Through this experience, the Holy Spirit showed me that my relationship to my son to this point was as the disciplinarian and not as one who gives encouragement and positive reinforcement. Instantly, I knew that if I didn't work to change our relationship, I would lose my son forever. I would need to win my son back to me by spending concentrated time with him on a regular basis.

I am so happy that children are so quick to forgive and forget. After only about two outings, Jonathan and I developed a precious and loving relationship that has continued to this day. I have repeated this process with each of my four children during the last thirteen years, and it has proven to bear good fruit.

I realize through this experience how grateful I am that God's love for me is not merely as a disciplinarian but mainly as a loving, tender, encouraging Father who leads me by His tender love.

By the way, I'm in technical work again. We're all much happier.

I pray, Father,
that the fathering You've put in me
will bring glory to Your name
and cause all of my children to set their faces like a flint
to follow in Your ways.
Amen.

The integrity of the upright guides them,
but the unfaithful are destroyed by their duplicity.

Proverbs 11:3, NIV

A Priceless Jewel

John Strubhar

Integrity has received a *bad rap* due to the brouhahas and snafus in the lives of men in almost every sector of society. It seems we're more aware of scandal in people's lives than we are of integrity!

Integrity means telling the truth all the time and not altering the truth for personal manipulation or advantage. It's a life totally open before God. It means we let others hold us accountable to the blind spots that may exist in our personal and professional lives.

I believe integrity is the indispensable ingredient, an unqualified extra that sets a man on the cutting edge spiritually. Take away integrity and you're left with hypocrisy.

Integrity is not born in a crisis; it emerges firm in a crisis. The man of integrity will not have to convince others he has it. It will be self-evident. Even under the closest scrutiny, the man of integrity consistently delivers. He doesn't betray his trust.

The key to integrity is self-discipline. It is birthed within us as we are totally honest with God, ourselves, and others.

On the other hand, integrity passes us by when we are more focused on the actions of others than our own consistency. Integrity misses us completely when we're consumed with role-playing spirituality, rather than being spiritual men. Though outwardly we may be able to play the role successfully, internally our lives will be in shambles. We will race through life trying to cover our tracks only to discover our fraudulent lifestyle impacts everything we touch. No amount of self-talk will help. In our hearts, we know better.

Every day is an occasion for an integrity test. It may be given by a store clerk, our wives, our kids, or a colleague. When others have torn at our hearts with unfounded criticism, integrity will allow for the Lord's praise, "Well done," instead of personal castigation.

Integrity is the priceless jewel we must guard at all costs. Don't leave home without it!

Lord,
Your integrity cannot be equalled!
In my pursuit after You,
help me to safeguard my heart with all diligence.
When I'm distracted and tempted,
may my accountability to You alter my thought patterns
and return me to the "way of integrity."
Amen.

Each one should be careful how he builds...
His work will be shown for what it is.

1 Corinthians 3:10,13, NIV

Foundations for Progress

Paul P. Tell, Jr.

A small manufacturing business in our area began to struggle with declining sales. The owner started going to his shop floor after hours to run the machinery and put out more product. But he knew this was only a diversion. What he really needed to do was face the marketplace, see it clearly, and be creative and innovative. It made no sense to make a product if it wasn't selling. For this business, the underlying assumptions about the market were no longer applicable; the market had changed.

My experience with real estate development has brought similar lessons. Investing in improvements to a problem property may do nothing to increase its value. What's really needed is a realistic and practical examination. The present and future revenue from the property has to be assessed before anything more is done to it.

With many of my plans, I get a vision for a project and get excited about the pursuit of it. Then something happens. I learn about problems, complications, conflicts, or the real costs involved. Sometimes I discover my wife has other ideas, or the project isn't a good fit for our company.

As the reality of the situation takes hold, I have choices. I can stop, slow down, or forge ahead, knowing that the risk of failure increases if I'm not realistic about the real potential or suitability of the project.

Our future in heaven and Christ merits a reality check. Is my activity resting on a cloudy concept of God's goodness? Perhaps my attention is fixed more on church schedules, facilities, or other members of the congregation. For just a moment, I need to think about the underlying foundation of God's gift of an eternal relationship with Him in Christ, and ask, "Am I operating under realistic assumptions?"

Father,
I know You care most of all that I build for eternal success.
Thank You for the enjoyment of the pursuit.
Please have my work fit best with Your master plan for me.
Amen.

If thou doest well, shalt thou not be accepted?

Genesis 4:7, KJV

Those Aggravating Do-Gooders

Richie G. Thomas

The hardest thing about having a relationship with God is that He always has to have it His way. For example, remember that Cain and Abel thing? You remember the story: they brought sacrifices to God. Abel brought a lamb from his flock. He was a shepherd and his offering was accepted. Cain brought fruits and vegetables. He was a farmer but his offering was not accepted. Never mind the prophetic implications of the blood sacrifice, just put yourself in Cain's shoes. How embarrassing! Your younger brother gets "atta-boy" backslaps from God while your offering is ignored completely. Cain must have thought, "Why, if I had a club I'd…"

I identify more with Cain than Abel. I've always found it easier to criticize the successful than to be a success; especially after a failure. Insulated from the emotion of the situation and without the firsthand experience of the participants, I'm ready to give cheap advice to Cain.

"Grow up, dummy. If God wants a lamb, give Him a lamb. No big deal."

I went to my class reunion and saw my best high school friend. He was tan, thin, and rich. I wanted to kill him! I told myself on the way home that it's a virtue to be pale, fat, and poor. "After all," I reasoned, "I'm spiritual and he's not even religious."

I'm still in the process of learning the lesson Cain refused to learn. Even if I kill my successful brother, I have not freed myself from the obligation before God to succeed. What we desire most, acceptance and joy, comes only as the result of doing what's right.

Father,
teach me to enjoy my brother's success.
Teach me that criticizing my brother
does not diminish his success
nor does it make me successful.
Amen.

My flesh and my heart may fail, but God is the strength of my heart and my portion forever.

Psalm 73:26, NIV

A Record Week

Dennis E. Way

Monday was a holiday. My wife and I spent the whole day with friends, driving through the Napa Valley, picnicking, and generally having a really good time laughing and sightseeing. It was a great day. Then Tuesday arrived.

Tuesday was a disaster, and that's putting it mildly. I'm not sure exactly what caused it, or when my attitude started to change, but everything seemed to go wrong while I was at the wholesale auction looking for used cars for my lot. It seemed as if nothing worked the way I wanted it to. By the time I got home I was deep into self-pity. I was so bad, my good-natured wife, Carol, immediately sensed I was not someone that any reasonable person needed to deal with, so she gave me a lot of space that evening. I went to bed as out of sorts as I'd been earlier in the day.

When I got up for my usual devotional reading early Wednesday morning, everything changed. Psalm 73 put me back on track, speaking to me very clearly. I had slipped and lost my foothold just as the psalmist said. I had been envious of others. I was reminded that God is my counsel and will provide me with strength. My job is to stay near Him.

What was the result of this scriptural reminder for me? The next three days were so good that it amounted to a record week for Way's Auto Sales. God is really my refuge, just as the psalmist declared.

I'm aware that distractions can keep me from maintaining my focus on the Lord. I should expect that events that occur in my day can knock me off course. Fortunately, God knows we're liable to get sidetracked or become preoccupied with our problems. It's also fortunate that we can go to Him to get reenergized and get our lives redirected.

Lord,
keep my eyes focused on You and on Your Word.
Let me magnify Your name.
Amen.

I Can Still Work on You

Dick Williams

I was driving back to our apartment after my second job interview that day. It looked favorable that I would be offered employment by one of the companies. Having finished my second year of Bible school, I was employed that summer as a sign painter, but I was discontent. As I headed home I heard something I will never forget. The Holy Spirit said to me, "Go ahead. I can still work on you."

I was frustrated with my present work. It seemed that no matter how hard I tried, I was unable to satisfy the high standards of my boss. I had never liked to paint, anyway, because of all the cleanup that was required; the brushes had to be free of paint or they would become stiff and useless.

My wife, Karen, and I had prayed that our Lord would provide me with a job for the summer. So when I was hired to paint signs, we knew it was a provision of the Lord. I had grown up working hard, so I really tried to give it my best. Yet the whole summer was filled with the testing of my faith. Not only was my boss constantly correcting my work, but also I frequently received a check that represented less than forty hours a week, when he had promised me full-time work. Finally, I said to myself, "Who needs all this grief? I'm going to look for another job."

Somehow the fact that we had prayed and believed that this job was from the Lord was overshadowed by the trials I was experiencing. The job was not the only trial I was going through. We were trying to save money for school, and Karen had been in the hospital twice that summer, first with an emergency appendectomy, then with a miscarriage. Since we didn't have medical insurance, we had medical bills that would take several months to pay.

Sure, I was feeling sorry for myself in deciding to look for another job. I had lost sight of the reality that trials in the hand of the Lord become the work of the cross in our lives. My eyes were on my circumstances, and I wanted relief from the pressures I was facing. So I decided to change jobs, hoping my new boss would be easier to work for.

When the Holy Spirit reminded me that the Lord was working in the midst of my trials, I once again yielded to Him and discontinued my search for another job. I realized that no matter where I worked, there would still be circumstances that our Lord would use to bring needed changes in my life.

Lord Jesus,
forgive me for feeling sorry for myself
and not seeing Your hand using the adversities of life
to change areas in my character that are not like You.
Grant me the grace to embrace the work of the cross
and continue to give You thanks for the provision of the job
with its accompanying trials.
Amen.

So we are ambassadors for Christ,

since God is making his appeal through us;

we entreat you on behalf of Christ,

be reconciled to God.

2 Corinthians 5:20, NRSV

Agents of Reconciliation

James H. Harrison

The board meeting became a nightmare. Agitated people spoke with raised voices and emphasized their views with closed fists hitting the table. Since I was the one presenting newly discovered facts and held the unpopular view, I couldn't help but take it personally. The heated meeting climaxed when Don stood, pointed his finger at me, and said, "As for you, I don't want to see your face for six months!" He turned, walked out the door, and slammed it shut.

With that act of hostility my heart fell into my stomach and I felt ill. I was so affected by his accusing finger and rejection that I wrote it down on my calendar and journal as "the board meeting from hell."

It's amazing how a word or action can fell the noblest idea or intention. Even more amazing is how the word or action kills something deep within the soul. I felt as if a part of my spiritual life had been amputated. I was no longer whole; a piece of me was missing. It left when Don walked out and closed the door to positive confrontation and the process of reconciliation.

The incident remained in my memory, but busy days at work, busy times with family, and my own mental defense mechanisms shoved the whole incident deep into the recesses of my mind. It would come to the forefront when Don and I happened to be at the same function, or when I was in stillness with prayer and meditation. It was during prayer when I ran across the journal entry and noticed the six-month anniversary was coming up. It was time to face it.

I prayed to God for boldness of spirit and words of reconciliation, went to Don's house, and knocked on the door. His face looked a little shocked when he opened the door and saw me. I said, "Don, it will be six months tomorrow."

He threw his head back in laughter and said, "Come on in."

Dear God,
give me the strength to stand in honor
and the courage to be an ambassador of Christ.
In His name I pray.
Amen.

Run in such a way as to get the prize.

1 Corinthians 9:24, NIV

Stop Running and Stopping

Paul P. Tell, Jr.

Aesop told a story about a race between a rabbit and a turtle. Of course we know the turtle won! How could that happen? Well, it was simple. The rabbit goofed off! He stopped for too long. He thought he had plenty of time and could take a nap before finishing the race.

It's like coming to the fifteenth of the month, with three-fourths of the month's work done, and giving in to the inclination to take it easy for a day or two. The pause feels okay because most of the month's goals have been reached. It can be a harmful delay.

Too often, I've started a project and then stopped. I didn't really mean to quit. I just wanted to take a break. Then my complacency allowed the break time to get sort of extended and extended and extended some more, until there wasn't enough time remaining to do the project right.

In the backyard of my home in northeastern Ohio, when it's sunny and warm, I sometimes write at a wooden picnic table. It's easy to lay down the pen or turn off the laptop computer and stretch out on a cot under a huge oak tree that must be over a hundred years old—just like

Aesop's hare. A lost afternoon has sometimes become a lost weekend, and some of the sparkling thoughts I intended to develop have faded beyond recall.

This stops being a problem for me when I realize I have to do God's assignments first and with His help. That really is the answer! I have to determine what work has been put on my to-do list by my own doing and then realize that all I need to be concerned with are the assignments from God—and to get those done first.

Father,
please help me to laugh at myself once in a while and rest in You.
Guide my work with Your gifts of health and strength,
skills and opportunity.
May I go all the way to the finish line,
doing what You have planned for me,
not stopping short because of lack of discipline or discouragement.
I want to hear, "Well done."
Amen.

Join with others in following my example, brothers, and take note of those who live according to the pattern we gave you.

Philippians 3:17, NIV

Somebody's Watching

Robert Busha

We were pouring a lot of energy into providing support for flood victims in the midwest. Our initial focus was a fundraising event—a big flea market and auction. About eight weeks of preparation finally came together on a Saturday in early October. Dozens of volunteers were involved.

As chairman of the coordinating committee, I was right in the middle of it all that day as I'd been fulltime for two months. I simply filled little gaps helping with whatever needed to be done . . . setting up tables and chairs, making signs, answering questions, unloading cars and trucks, cleaning up.

At the end of the day, a hard-working fellow named Peter and I drove our pick-up trucks around the city returning borrowed folding tables. At each stop we helped each other unload and took a few minutes to chat and catch our breath. It'd been a long day in a long week and by then we were both feeling weary. Somehow the topic of age came up and I revealed I was nearly fifty.

Peter was surprised. He said he'd been watching me all day and was impressed I didn't appear to be tired. He said, "I'm just thirty-four and I'm whipped. You're a great role model for me."

Now, guys, I'm sharing this not to boast or to point to some unusual endurance I may have for someone middle-aged. This is serious. I'm telling you because what struck me about Peter's comment was the fact that he'd been paying attention to what I'd been doing. And, within a week or so, the same message was delivered in several other conversations with men and women at church and with the flood relief group. We'd all had more than one comment about our work from people we might have thought couldn't care less about what we were doing.

The message was loud and clear: Whatever we say, whatever we do, it's being recorded for certain by God and probably by someone else as well. It may be our children or the neighbor kids or their parents or someone we work with, and the list goes on. However we're walking our Christian walk, however we're talking our Christian talk, we're setting an example at home, at work, and out in the community.

Think about it a second as I did. Who may be watching your walk and talk?

Lord,

I really do know I'm not alone on my journey with You.

Thanks for letting me know there may be someone else

who wants to come along

if I'm able to naturally reveal that the trip is worthwhile.

Keep me ever mindful of You.

Amen.

Meet Our Contributors

John Atherton and his family live in Rohnert Park, California. He and his wife, Pam, have one daughter, Holly, and two sons, Scott and Aaron. John's pastimes include music and gardening.

Terrance Barrett is originally from the Los Angeles area. He's now a fulltime student at Sonoma State University in Rohnert Park, California. Terrance loves books and browsing through bookstores.

Dan Benson and his family live in Fort Collins, Colorado. He is the author of *Man Talk: Making the Most of Your Work, Your Money, and Your Marriage.*

Charles Blaker is retired from the faculty of Brookstone School in Columbus, Georgia. He is published on a wide range of topics in newspapers and magazines, and is active in radio, television, theater drama, and modeling. Charles and his wife reside in Columbus.

James Bolton lives in Spokane, Washington, and is involved in nursing home ministry. He enjoys writing, theological studies, bicycling, racquetball, volleyball, and gardening. James is a member of the Evangelical Theological Society and the Washington Christian Writers' Fellowship.

Charles Brown works for a title insurance company, is an elder in his church, and is worship leader. He and his wife, Bobbie, have four children and live in Riverside, California. Charles is a charter member of the Inland Empire Writers' Guild.

Bob Busha focuses on leadership for individual and organizational development, especially in the church. He and his wife, Mary Catherine, live and work in Santa Rosa, California. Their life is almost totally consumed by helping bring books to life. Bob loves the mountains, the ocean, and hiking and backpacking in remote places.

Jerry Carr is pastor of Cornerstone Christian Fellowship Church in Boulder, Colorado, and a production and technical services coordinator for NeoData, Inc. Jerry and his wife, Carla, have two grown children, Lance and Teresa.

Tom Carter is the author of more than fifty articles and seven books, including *What Believers Must Know to Grow* and *For Members Only: A Guide to Responsible Church Membership*. He is the compiler and editor of *Spurgeon at His Best*. Tom is a pastor who lives with his wife, Mary, their two daughters, and one son in Dinuba, California.

Tim Coyle is pastor of Grace Brethren Church in Newark, Delaware, and an instructor at Truth Bible Institute. He is active with the Delaware Family Foundation. He and his wife, Mary, live in Bear, Delaware. He enjoys gardening (vegetables and roses), and has a special love for dogs, especially golden retrievers.

Jack Edwards and his wife, Betty, live in Santa Rosa, California. Jack is retired from the California Highway Patrol and currently works as a private investigator. His hobbies include bow hunting, golfing, and woodworking. Jack and Betty have served with Youth with a Mission (YWAM).

Bernie Epperson is the shipping and receiving supervisor for a company in Oneida, New York. He enjoys writing, drama, gardening, softball, and working with teens. Bernie performs Christian satirical sketches for church and community groups.

James Harrison lives in Rancho Cordova, California. He is president of the Sacramento Christian Writer's Club, and he records taped books for the learning disabled and blind. Jim has taught in elementary school and served as pastor in United Methodist churches in Nevada and California.

David Hauk is an optometrist in group practice and lives in Reading, Pennsylvania, with his wife, Debra, and their three children. In addition to collecting foreign and ancient coins, and getting more serious about his writing, the majority of Dave's free time is taken up with his family . . . and he loves it.

Jack Hayford is senior pastor of The Church on the Way in Van Nuys, California. He is an avid reader and pianist and is the composer of over four hundred published songs. His books include *The Heart of Praise, I'll Hold You in Heaven, Moments with Majesty, Rebuilding the Real You, Restoring Fallen Leaders, Taking Hold of Tomorrow,* and *Worship His Majesty.*

Oren House and his wife of forty-five years, Grace, live in Spokane, Washington. His published articles include "The Bottle on My Dresser," "When the Savior Becomes a Stranger," "Why Do We Hide," and "Out of the Pit." Oren is a retired office manager. He's spent nearly fifty years teaching adult Sunday School and preaching in small churches, rescue missions, and jails.

R. Kent Hughes is senior pastor of College Church in Wheaton, Illinois. He is a prolific author and he and his wife, Barbara, have four children. He has written *Disciplines of Grace, Disciplines of a Godly Man, Abba Father: The Lord's Pattern for Prayer, Living on the Cutting Edge,* and *Liberating Ministry from the Success Syndrome.*

Bill Hybels is pastor of Willow Creek Community Church in South Barrington, Illinois. He was also chaplain of the Chicago Bears for five years. He is the author of *Honest to God? Becoming an Authentic Christian, Too Busy Not to Pray,* and *Christians in a Sex-Crazed Culture.*

Michael Martin and his wife and two teenage boys live in Fairfax, Virginia. He enjoys running, hiking, nature, and sports, and working for environmental organizations. Mike is a lawyer and new writer. His work has been published in *The Upper Room.*

Chris McMinn is the pastor of The City of Truth Christian Center in Santa Rosa, California. He relaxes with reading, writing, and walking. Chris and his wife, Betsy, and their three sons reside in Santa Rosa.

Lt. Col. Louis Merryman (USAFR, Ret.) loves to watch movies and to write plays, devotionals, and other articles, many of which have been published and performed. His latest play is *Ernie and the Christmas Angels*. He also likes hot air ballooning. Louis lives in El Segundo, California.

Al Munger and his wife live in Poulsbo, Washington. He retired a few years ago after serving as a pastor for thirty-two years. Al has written for *Viewpoint* magazine. He enjoys RV travel, photography, woodworking, and radio-controlled airplanes. Al is pastor-in-residence at Northwest College in Kirkland.

Eric Nishimoto is a freelance illustrator and writer living in Thousand Oaks, California, with his wife, Adrienne, and their two children. He is the author of various inspirational articles in local and denominational Christian periodicals. He teaches Christian social ethics, leads home-based Bible studies, and participates in ministries for the poor and homeless.

Lloyd John Ogilvie is senior pastor of the First Presbyterian Church of Hollywood, California. He and his wife, Mary Jane, have three children. He is the author of several books, including *The Autobiography of God, You Are Loved and Forgiven, You Can Pray with Power,* and *A Future and a Hope*.

Ron Redmon lives in Guerneville, California, with his wife, Joyce, and their children, Lisa and Evan. Ron is a registered nurse in the oncology ward at Santa Rosa Memorial Hospital. He and Joyce are the adult caregivers for a church youth group.

Harold Sala is founder and president of Guidelines, Inc., an international Christian ministry reaching into more than eighty countries through radio, television, seminars, and books. His spare-time pursuits include tennis, golf, and biking. He and his wife, Darlene, make their home in Mission Viejo, California. Harold's recent books include *Today Can Be Different* and *Coffee Cup Counseling*.

Brad Sargent likes operatic whistling, puns, making people laugh, and hunting for out-of-print books. He lives in San Rafael, California, and is director of research for Exodus International, a worldwide network of Christian ministries. Brad serves on the board of directors of Christian AIDS Services Alliance.

Giles Scott is the service manager for an office products company in Santa Rosa, California, where he and his wife, Judy, live with their four children, Jonathan, David, Mary, and James. Giles has one hobby: his family. They like to camp on the northern California coast and fool around with their new computer.

Robert Smith is pastor of Calvary Baptist Church in Compton, California. He has written numerous magazine articles and has recently contracted with the National Baptist Convention to publish his book *The Hebrew Names for God*, and with Baker Books for his book *Blacks and Cults*. He and his wife, Margaret, live in Pasadena. Robert loves church league basketball, reading, and writing.

John Strubhar is senior pastor at Brookside Church of Fort Wayne, Indiana. He has written numerous magazine articles, has co-authored *Evangelistic Preaching: A Step by Step Guide to Pulpit Evangelism*. He and his wife, Sandra, have three daughters. John's pastimes include golf, tennis, and reading.

Paul Tell is part of a family business developing warehousing and manufacturing properties. He is the publisher of Telcraft Books, a small press for children's books. Paul is the author of the books *Fun with Aesop, Eternal Family*, and *Life: The Ribbon of Time*. Paul is a lay minister in the Akron, Ohio, area where he and his wife, Debra, have three married sons and three grandchildren.

Richie Thomas and his wife, Reba, live in Burton, Michigan, where he is the senior pastor at Faith Tabernacle, a metropolitan church enjoying rapid growth. Richie likes music, writing, and amateur sports, and is a fan of hot weather and wide fairways.

Ray Veal is an adaptive technology assessment clinician. Ray and his wife, Mary Rose, and their children live in Windsor, California. His hobbies include desktop publishing, reproducing antique furniture, and general woodworking.

Dennis Way is the owner of Way's Auto Sales in Windsor, California, where he and his wife, Carol, reside. They have two grown children and two grandchildren. Dennis is a deacon in Grace Fellowship Church in Santa Rosa.

Don White is a semi-retired pastor and missionary who spends much of his time writing technical manuals for Christian schools, traveling, and doing yard work. He and his wife, Ellen, live in Hillsboro, Ohio. They have four grown children living in Alaska.

Gene Wilder is pastor of the First Baptist Church in Fitzgerald, Georgia. He and his wife, Patricia, and their two teenage children live in nearby Lizella. In addition to his writing, Gene likes reading, skiing, golfing, and singing, as well as music composition and performance.

Dick Williams is the pastor of Grace Fellowship in Santa Rosa, California. Dick and his wife, Karen, are the parents of six grown children. When Dick has spare time he likes to fill it with photography, sailing, skiing, backpacking, and reading.

Credits